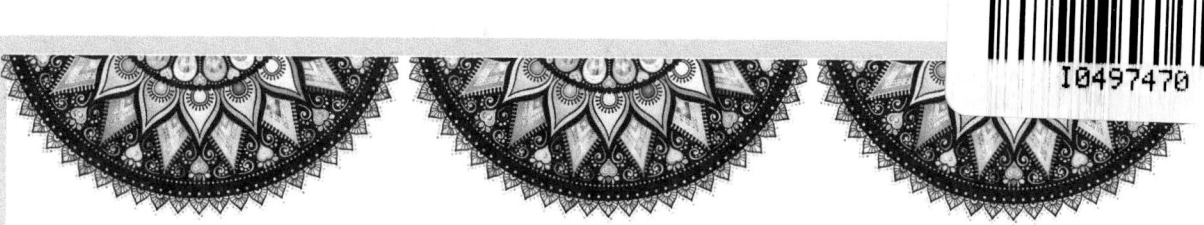

The mandala, or the so-called art of joy, is one of the arts available to everyone, does not require study or artistic talent, if it happens and you have a white paper in front of you at the time of your mind or talk on the phone or you get bored, in most cases you will find that the paper has been filled with drawings and art forms This indicates your eligibility to draw a mandala.

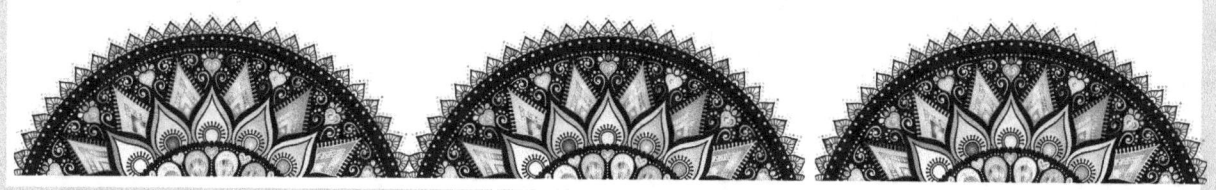

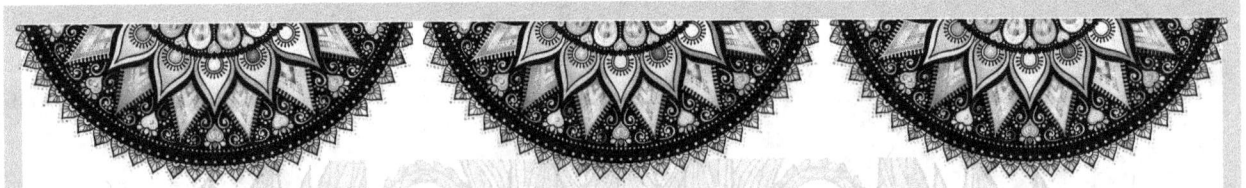

It is a circle in which the different geometrical circles and shapes are repeated, and the deeper the painter deepens in his circle, the more he reaches a deep inner focus and calm, so that you feel a strong attraction between the painter and his circle, attracting his eyes, his heart, his thoughts and his concentration, but calling him the art of joy, because he enters pleasure and joy on the soul Therefore, it is considered one of the arts that has been scientifically proven to play a positive role in dealing with stress resulting from the pressures of life.

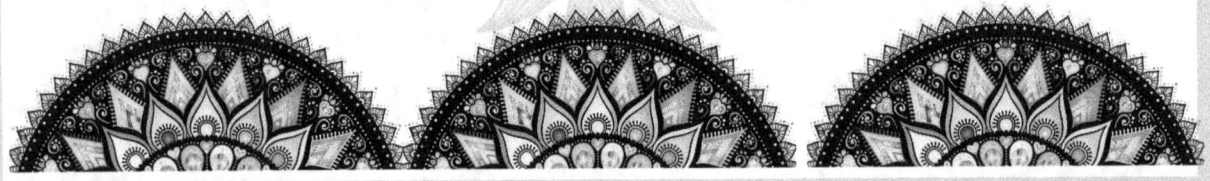

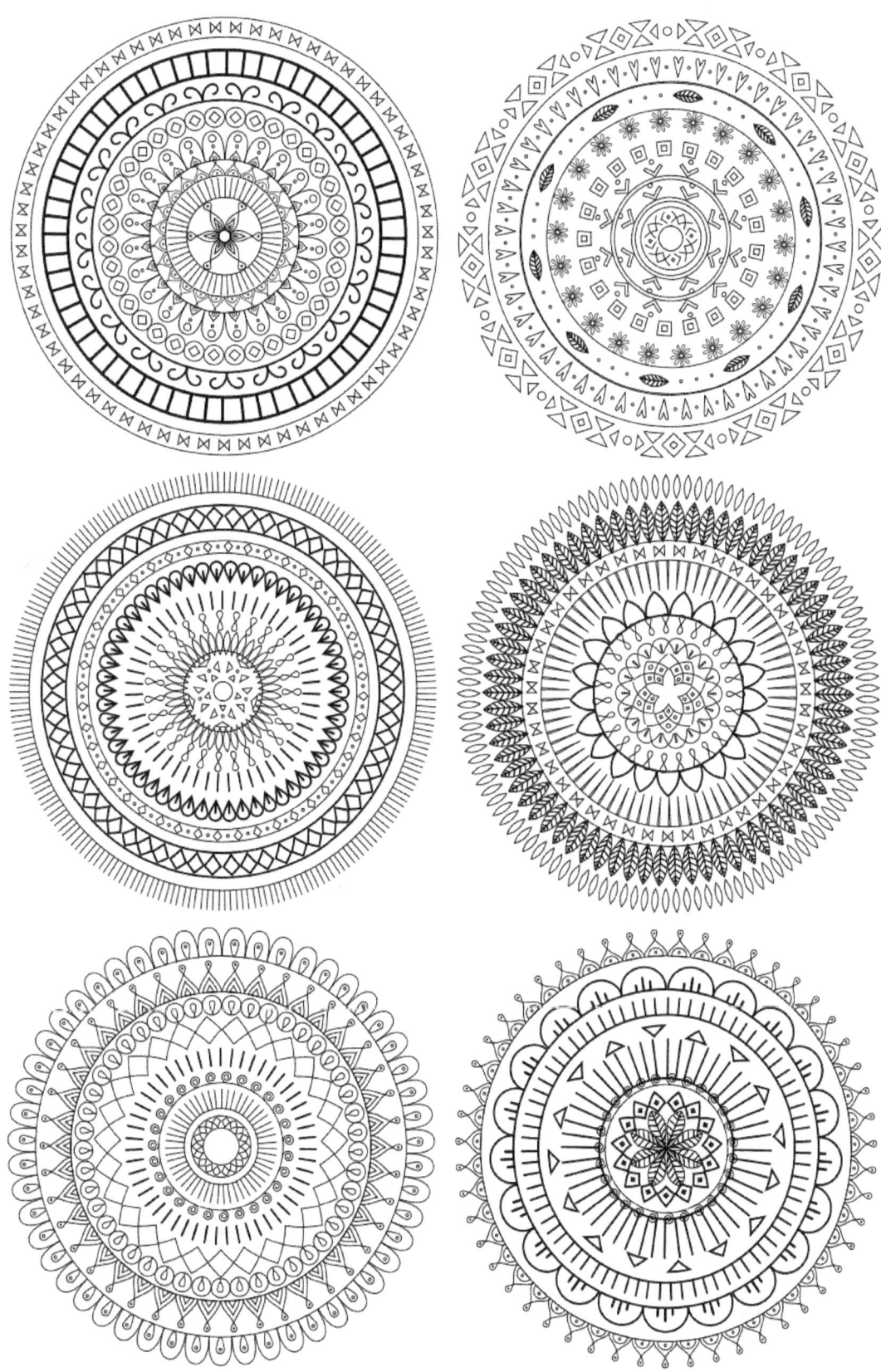

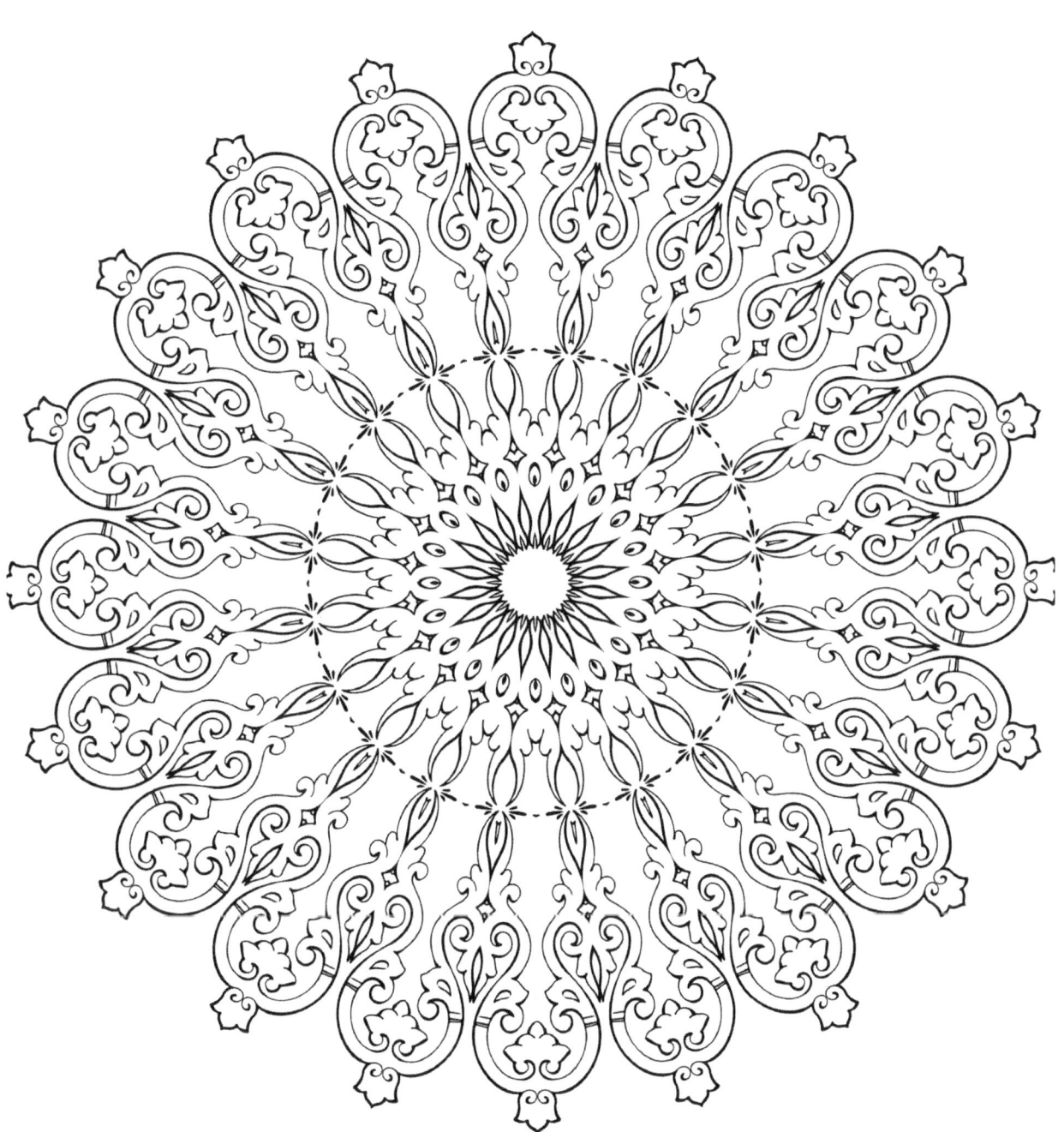

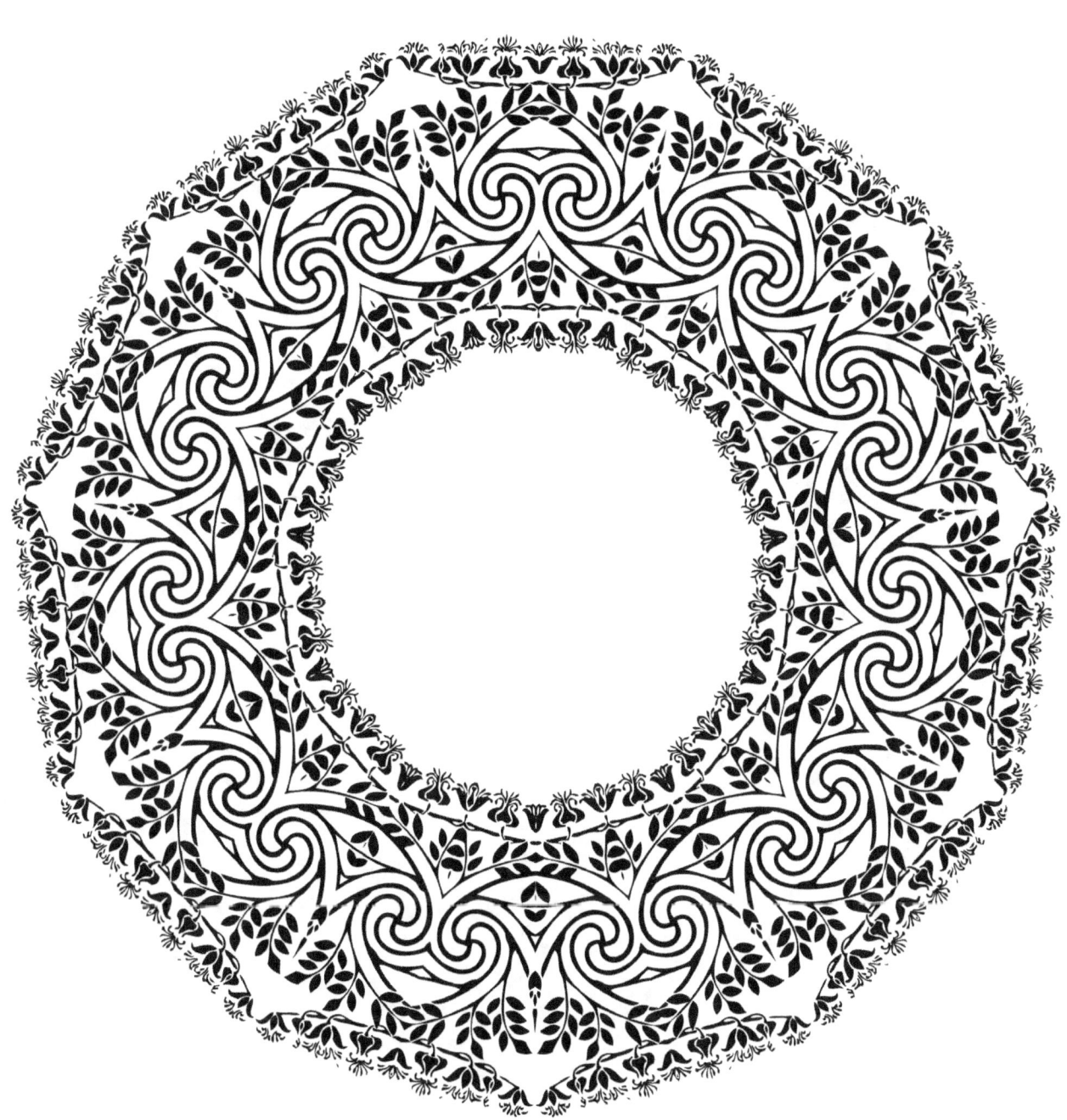

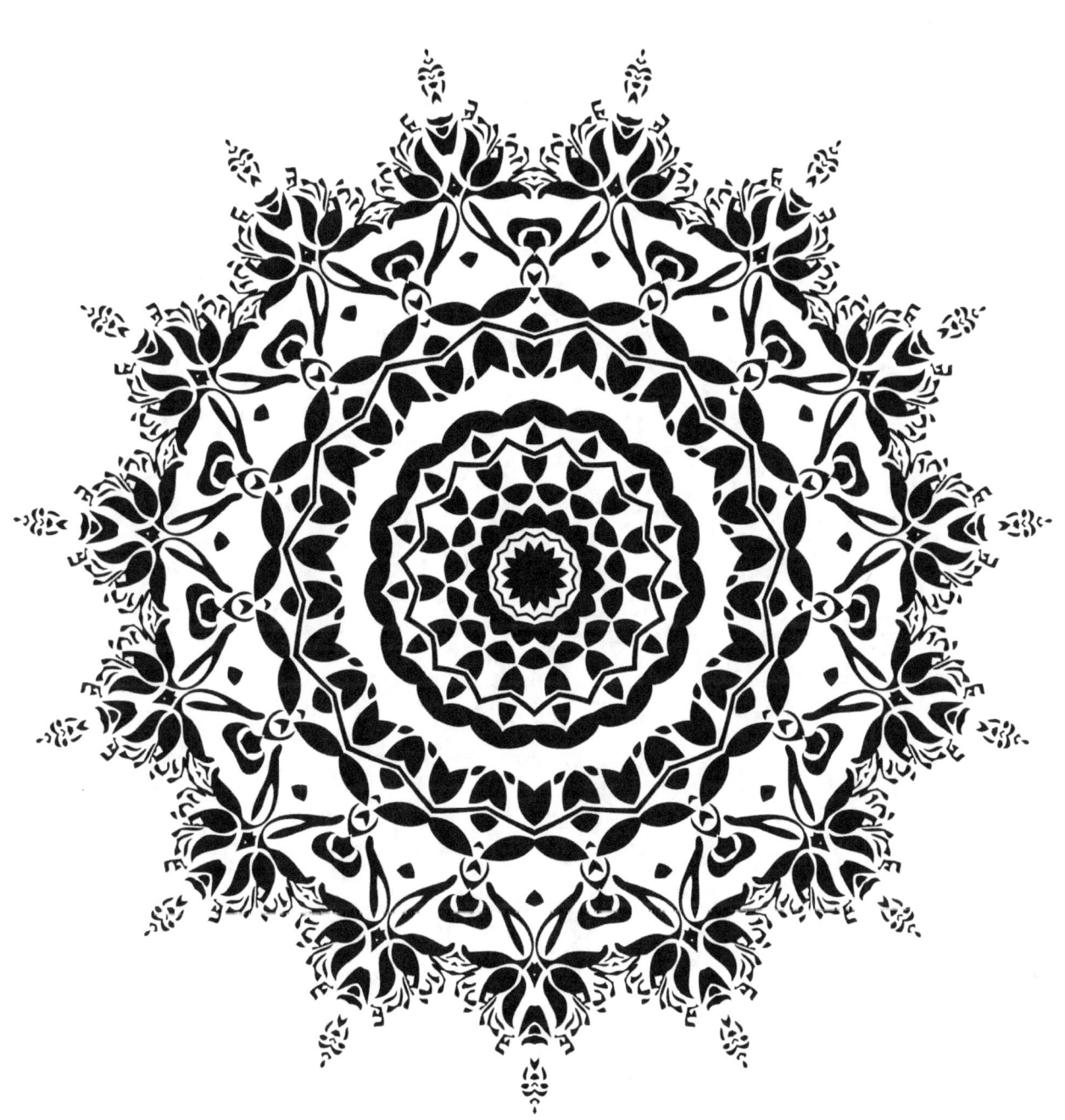

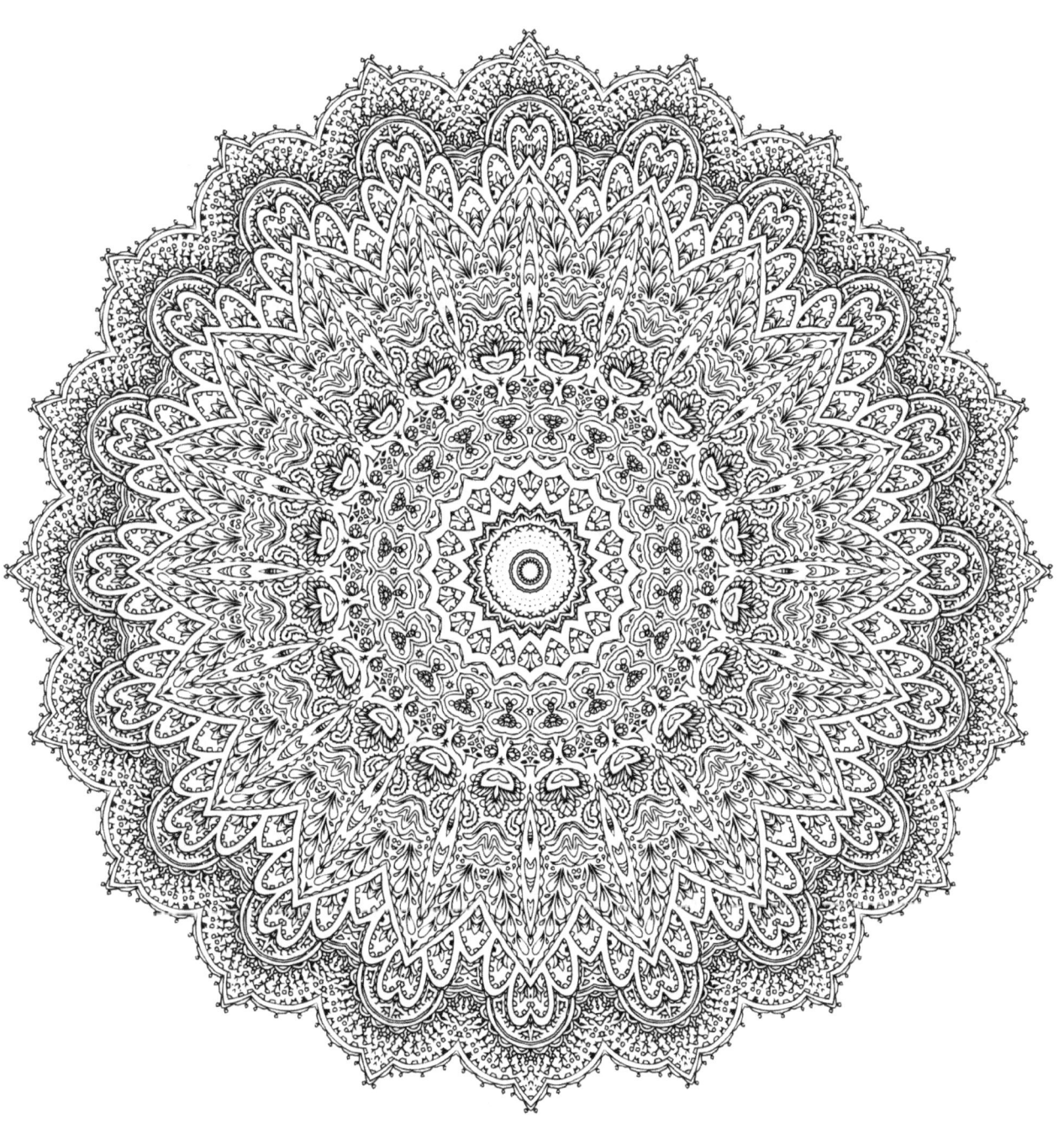

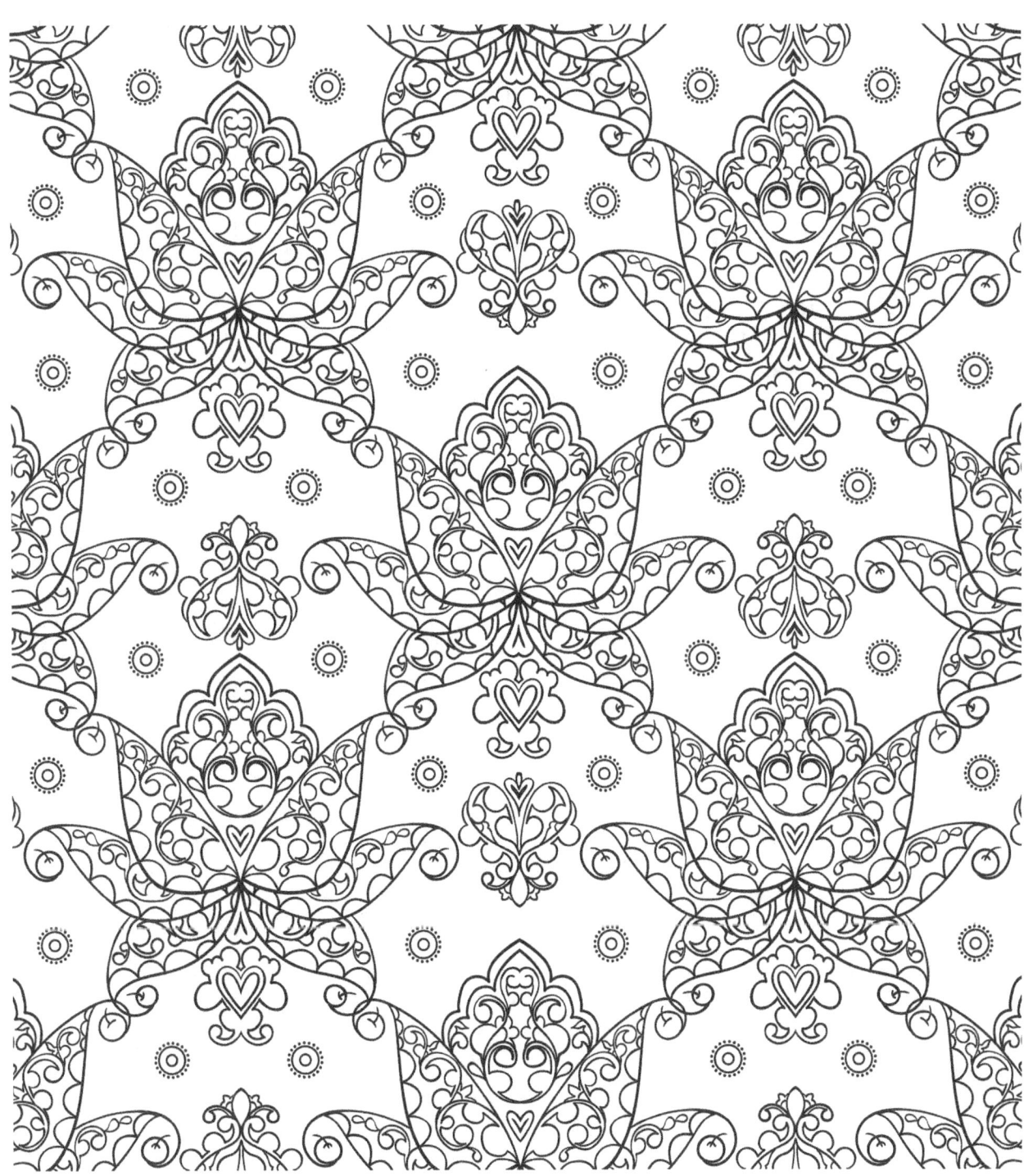

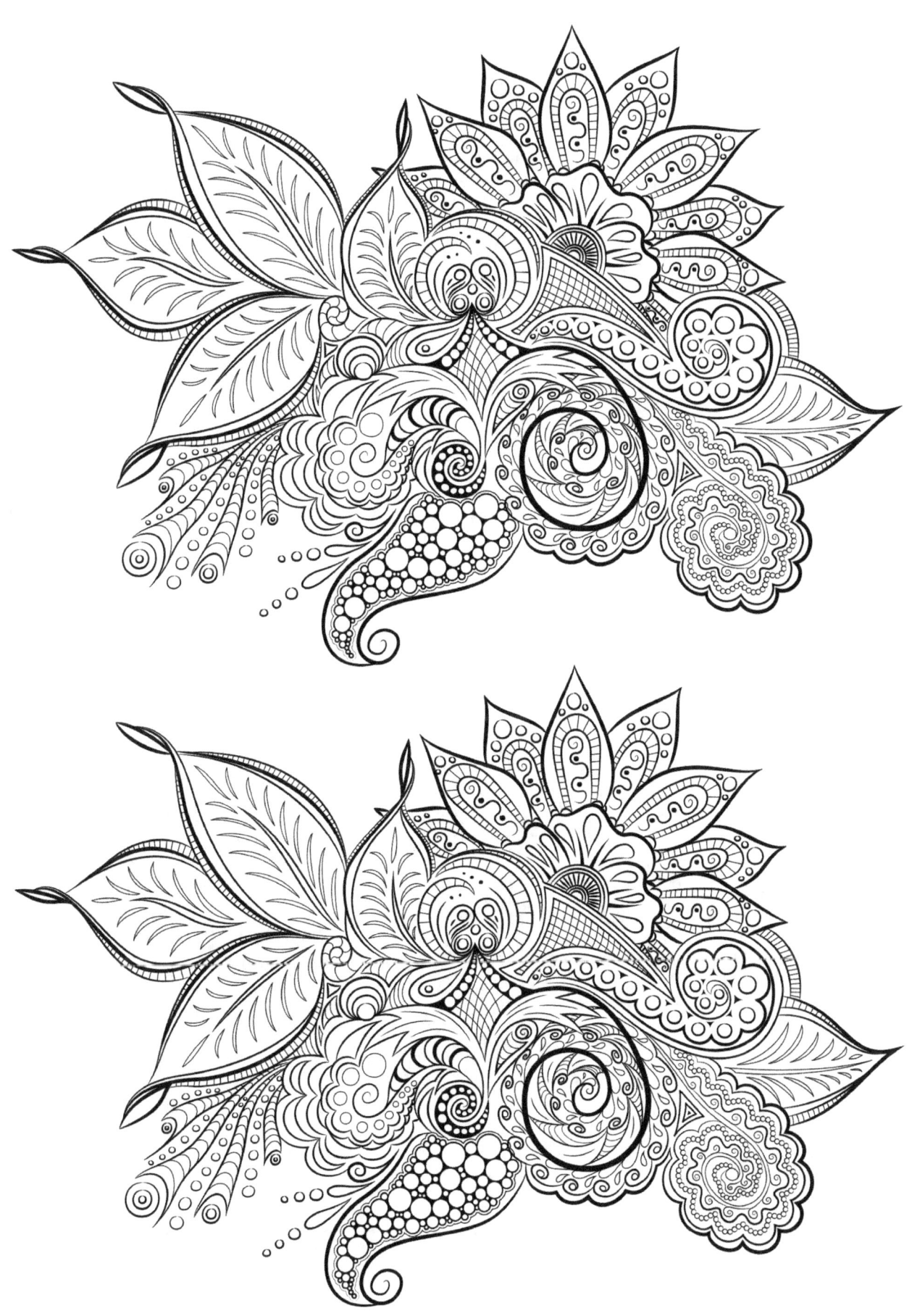

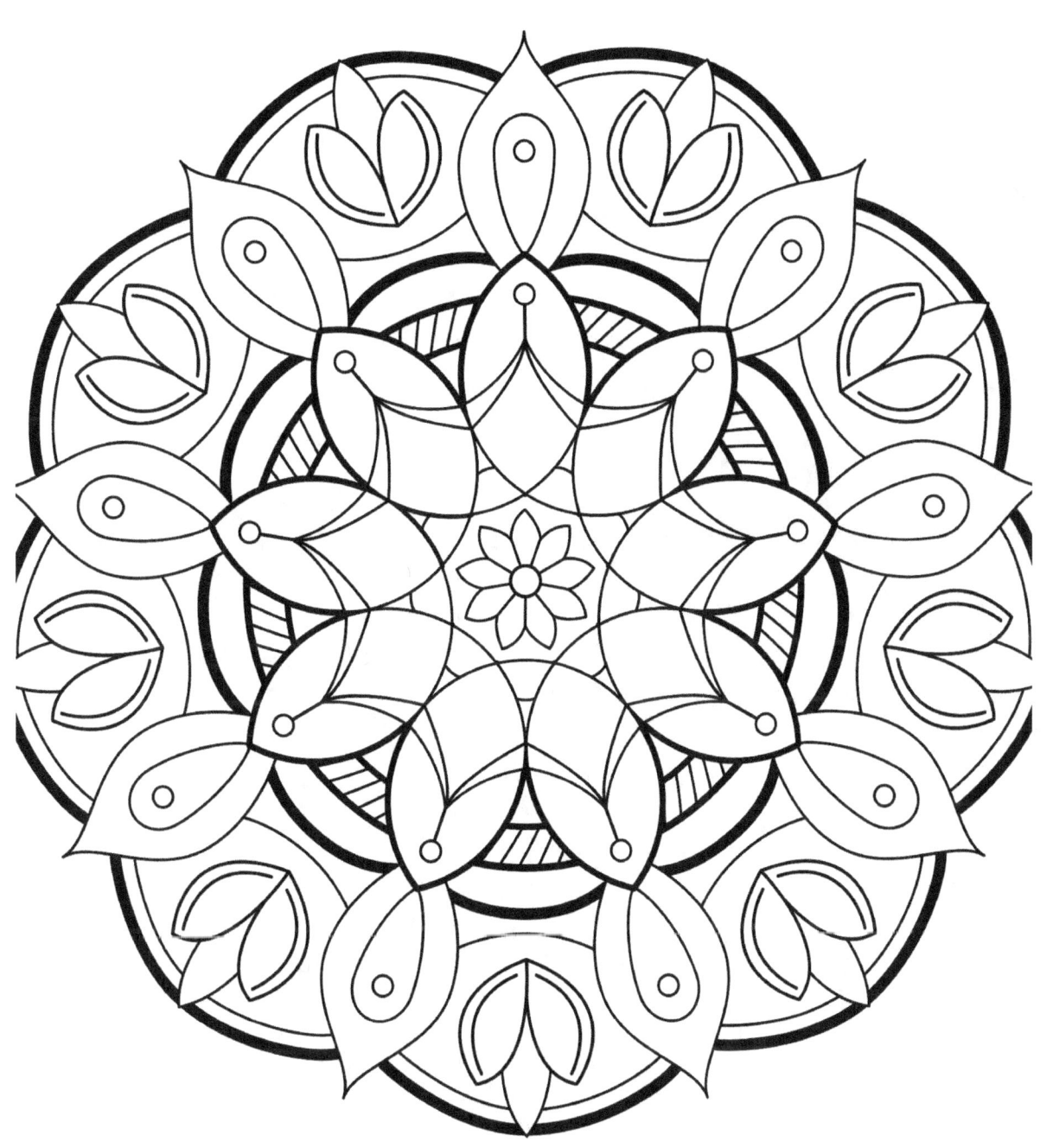

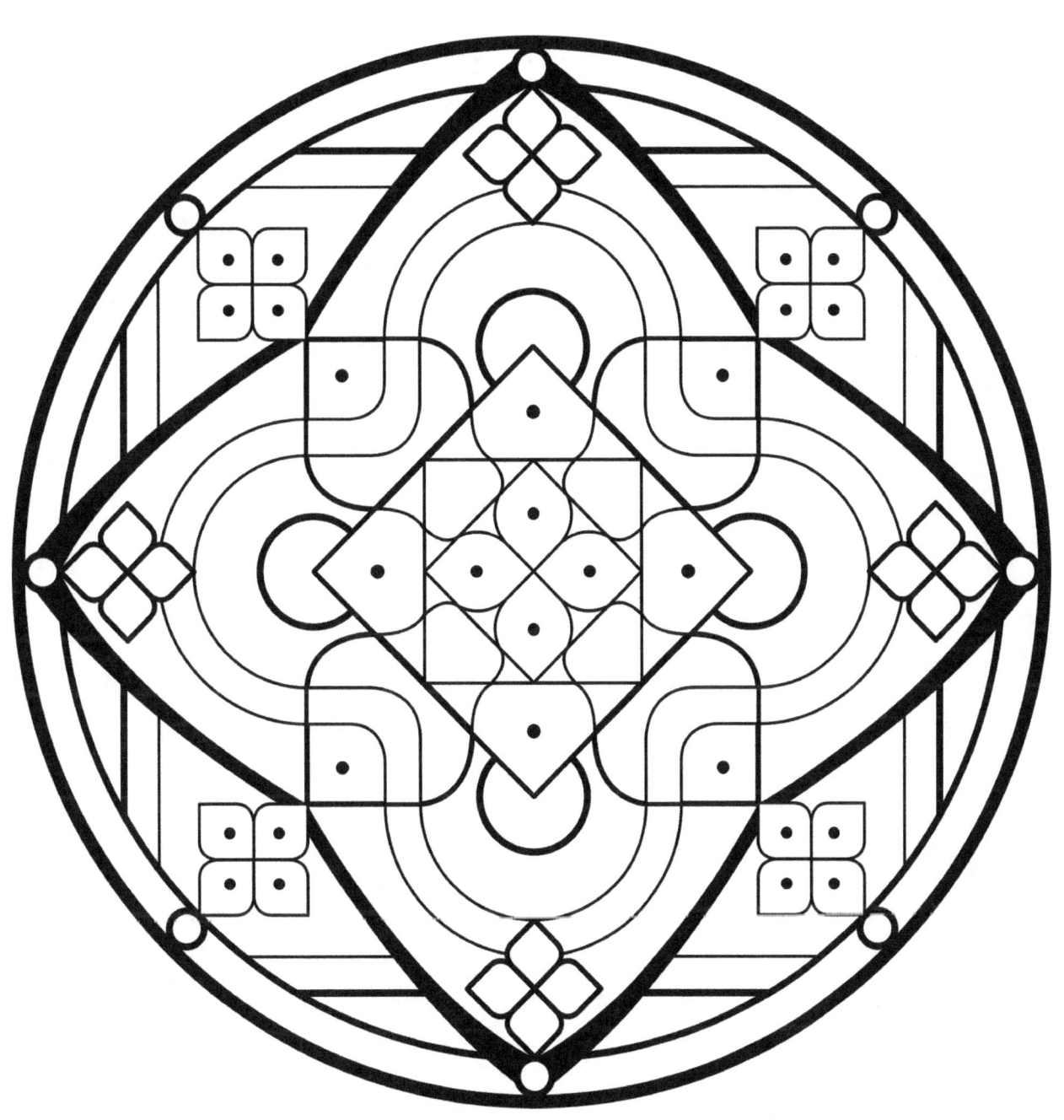

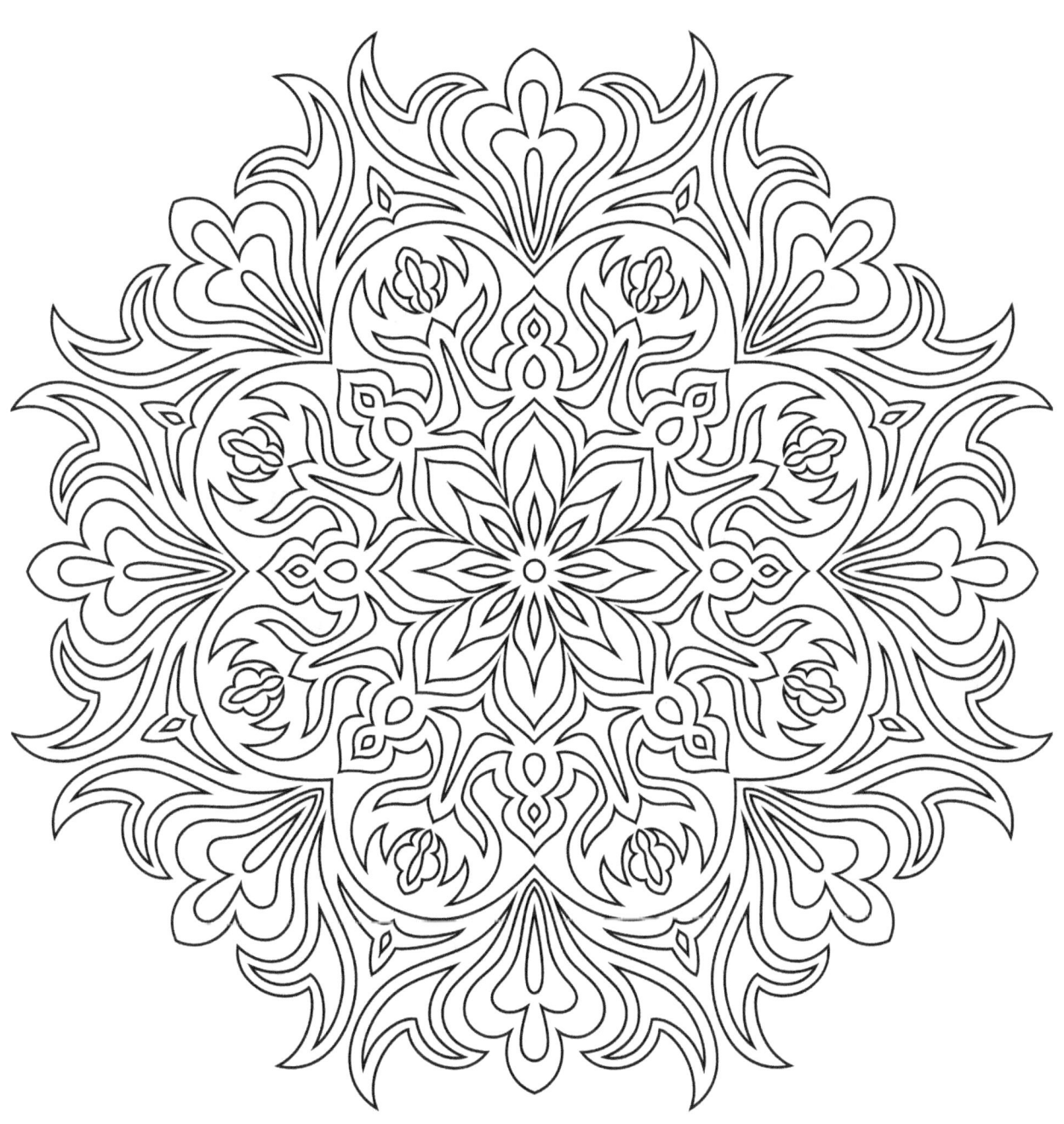

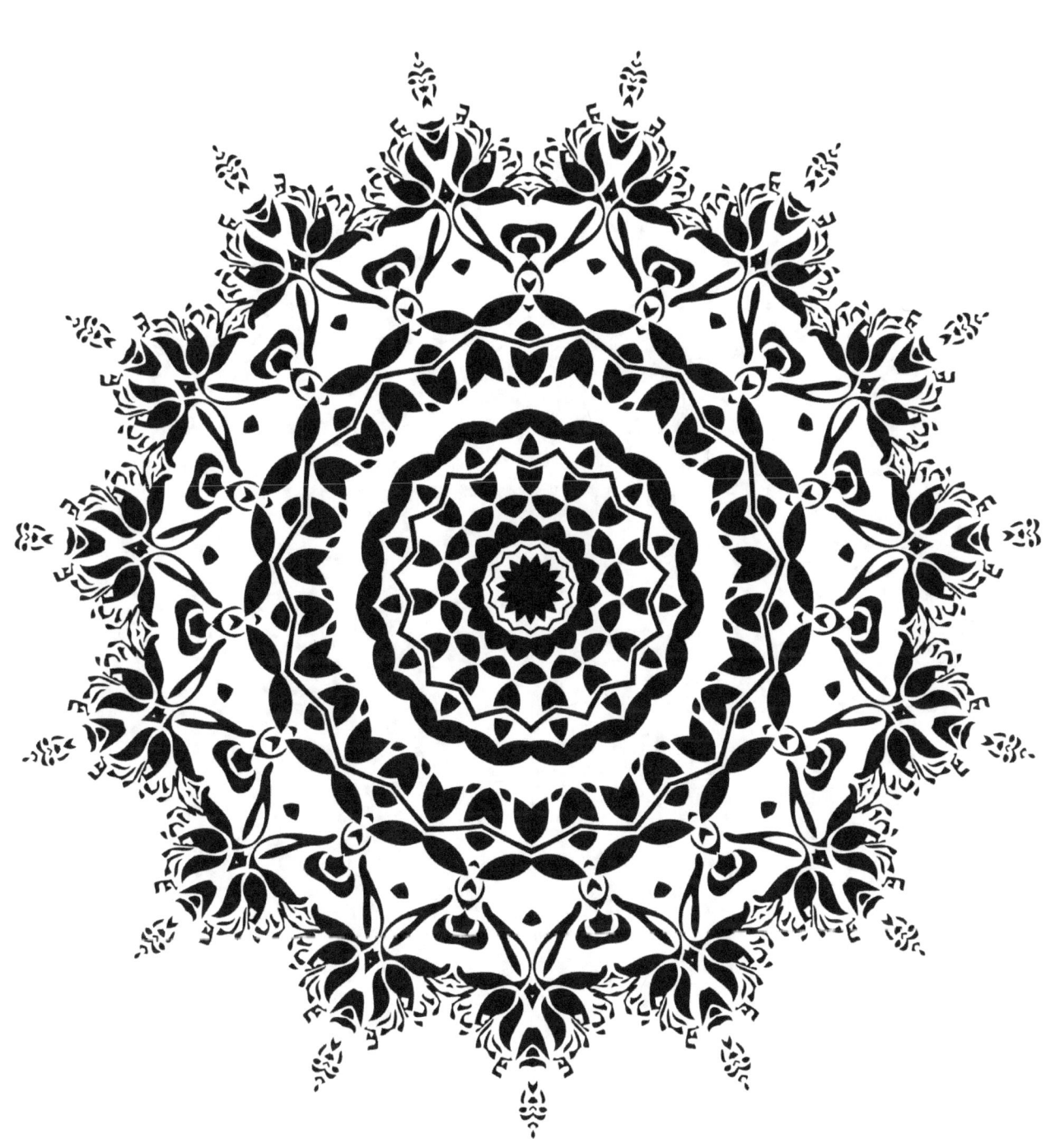

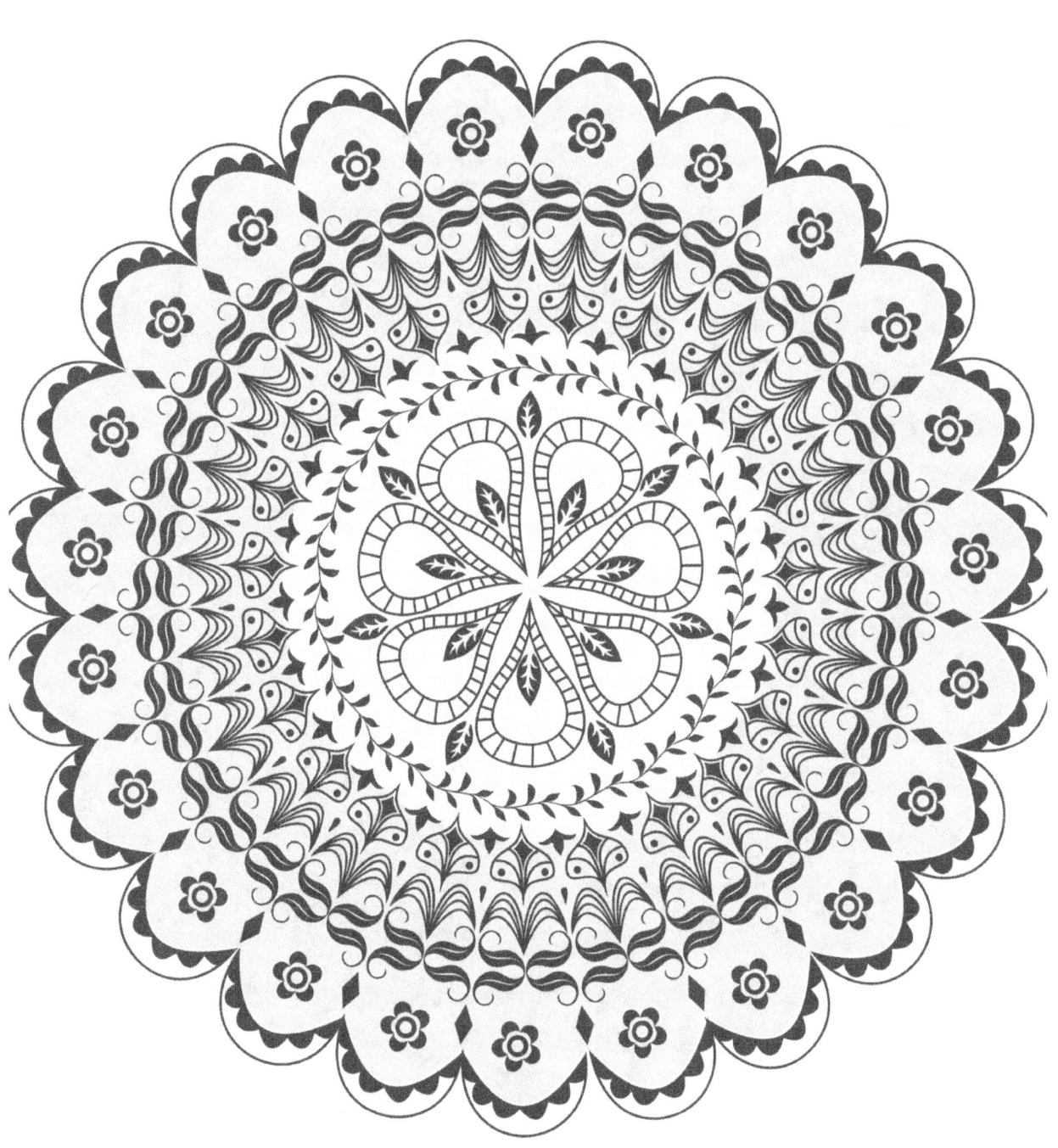

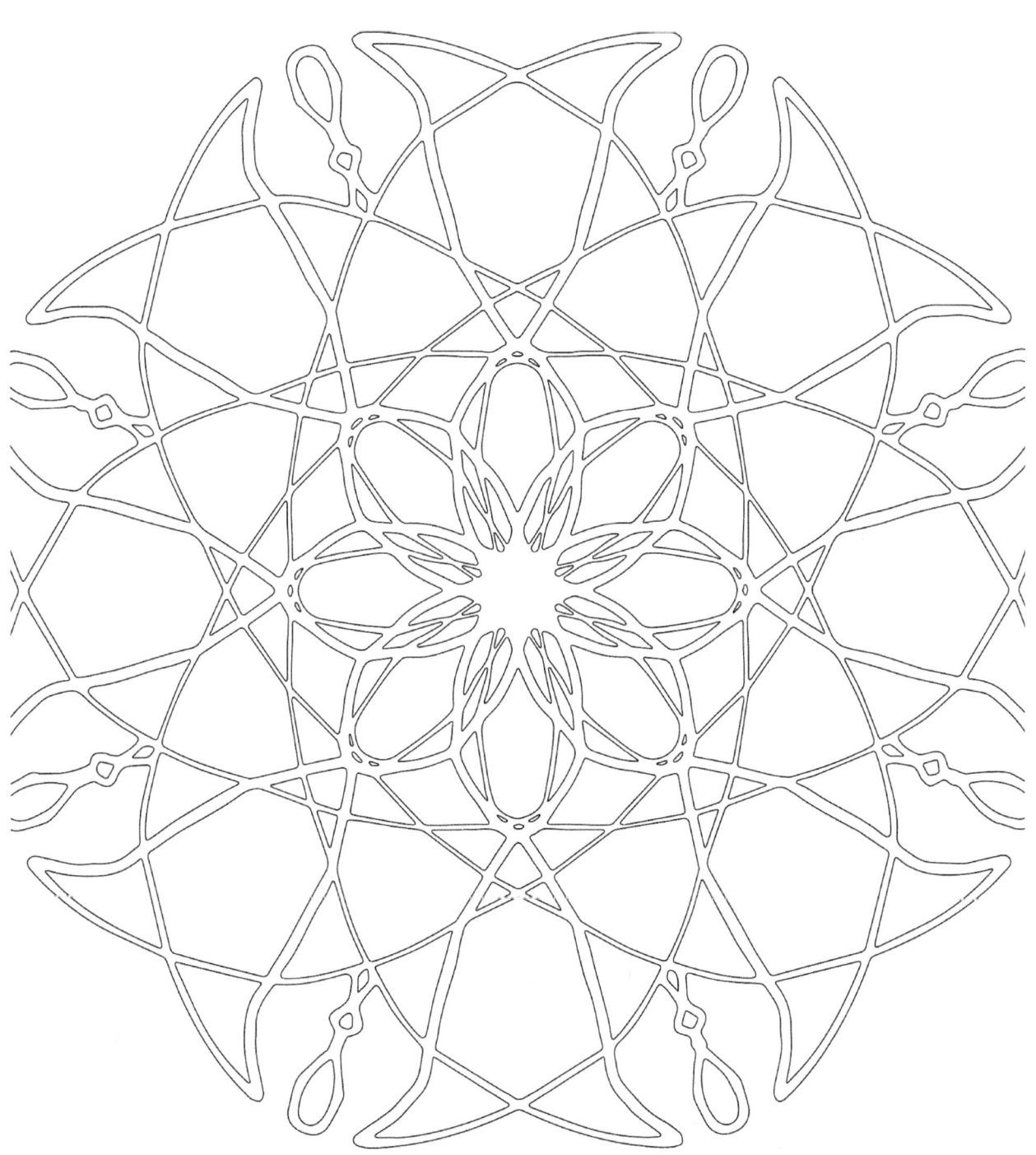

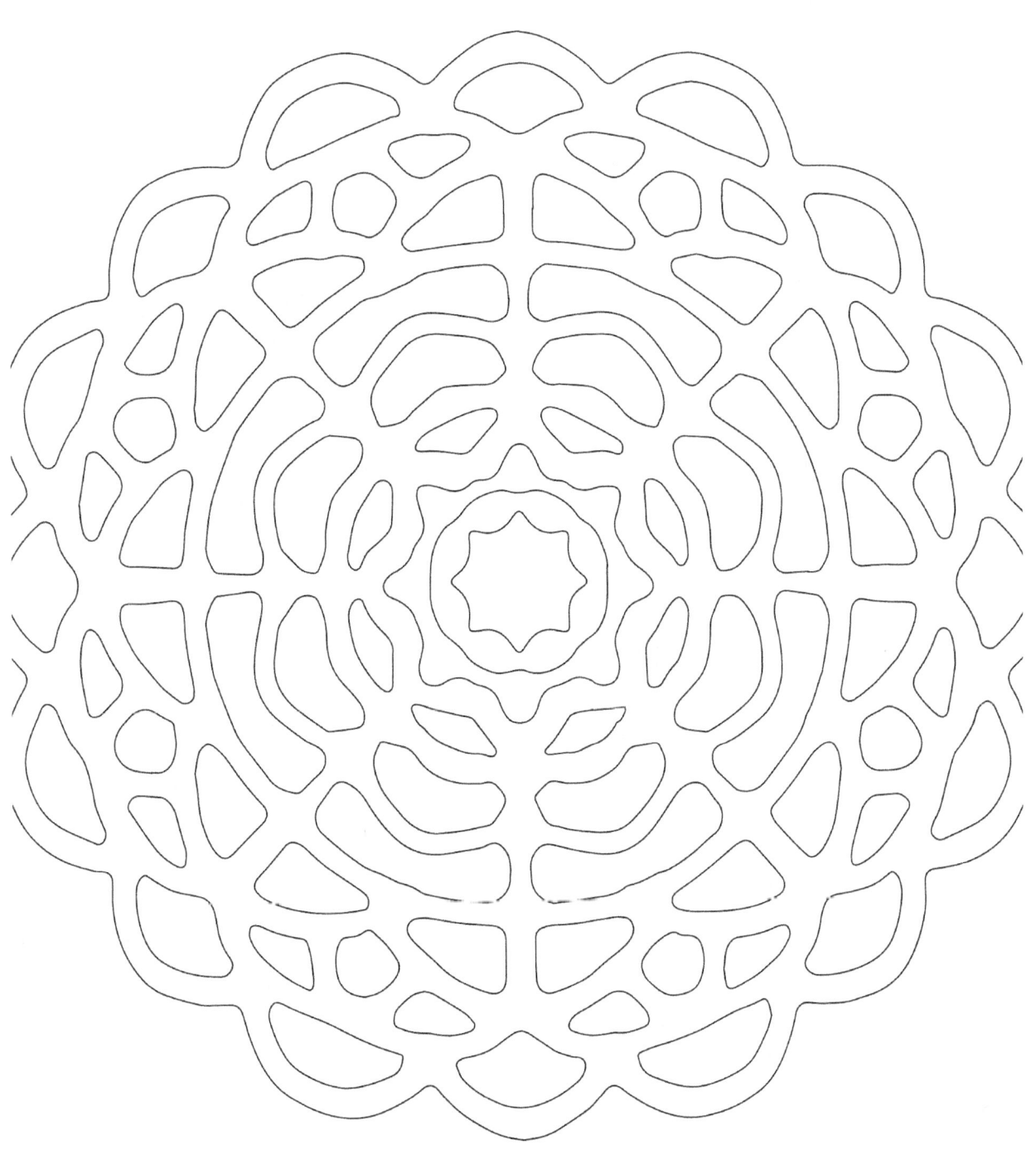

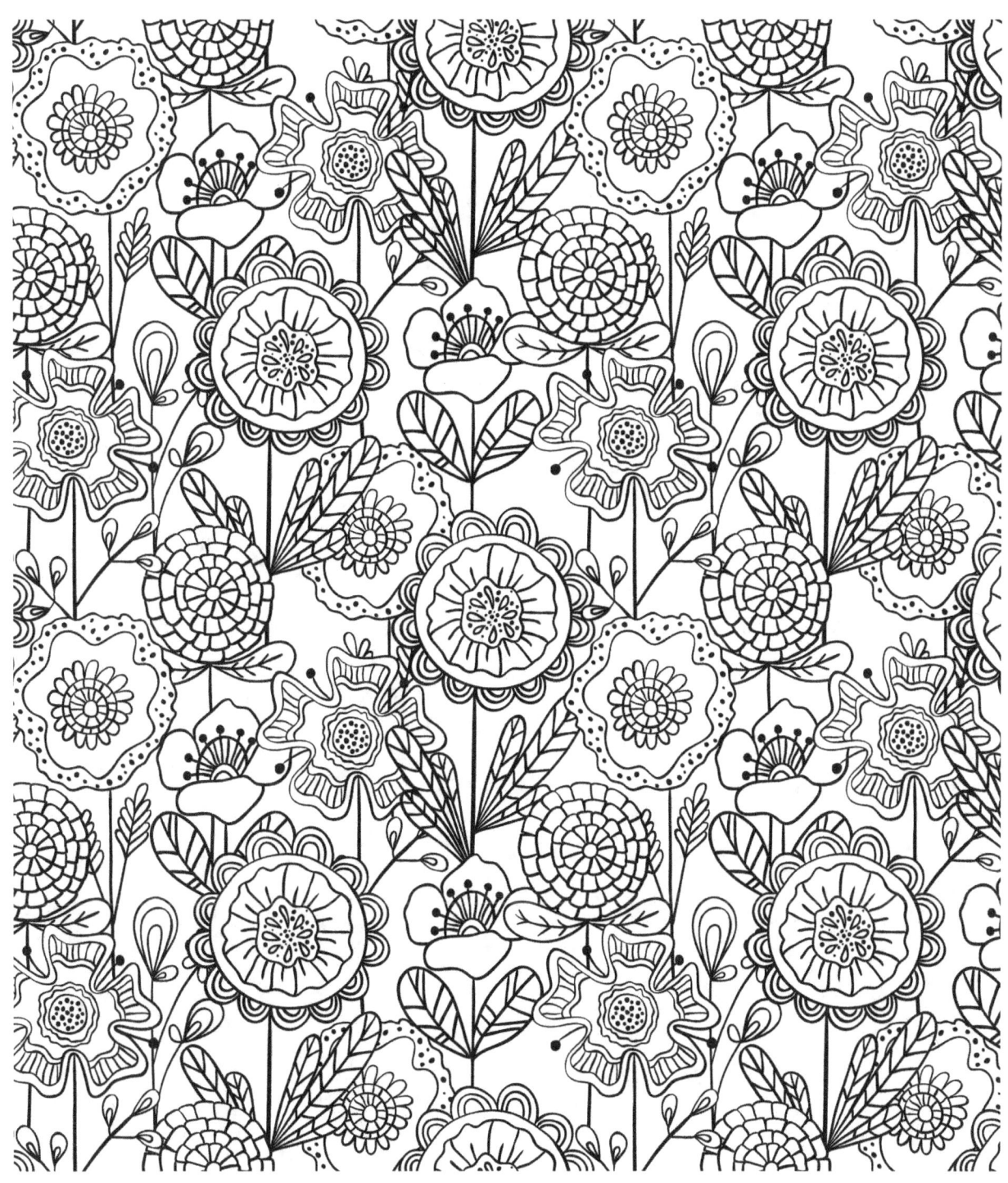

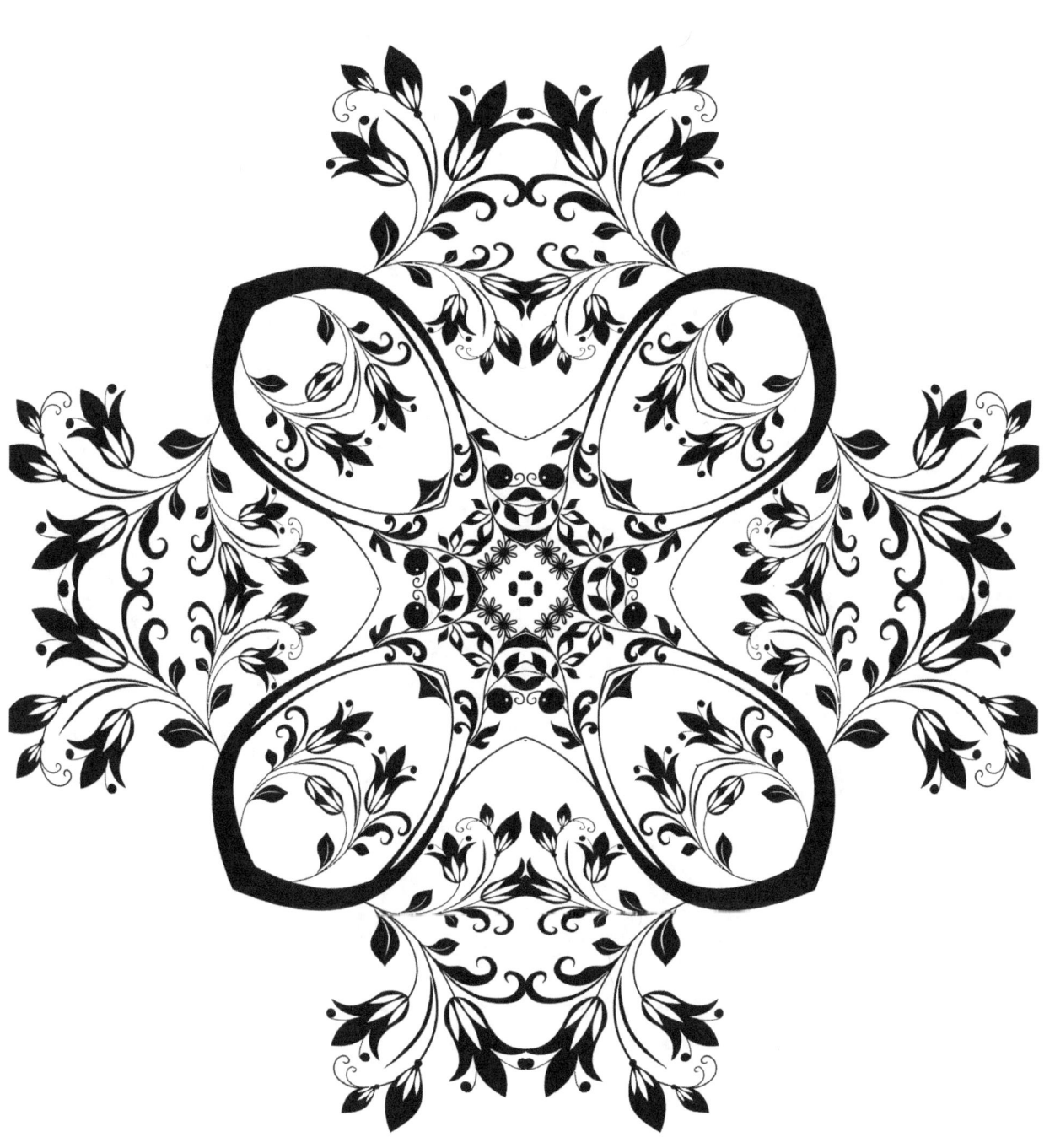

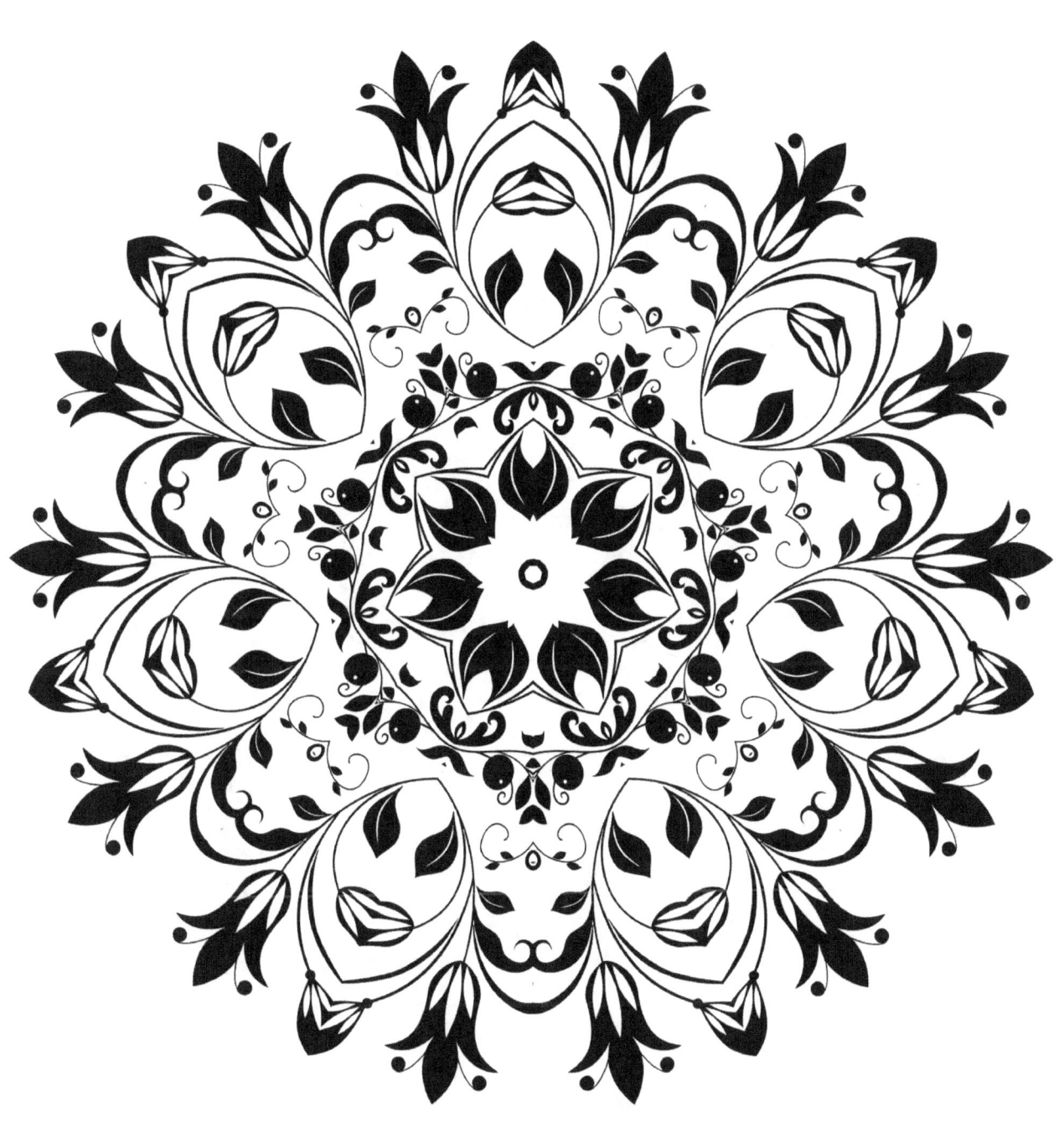

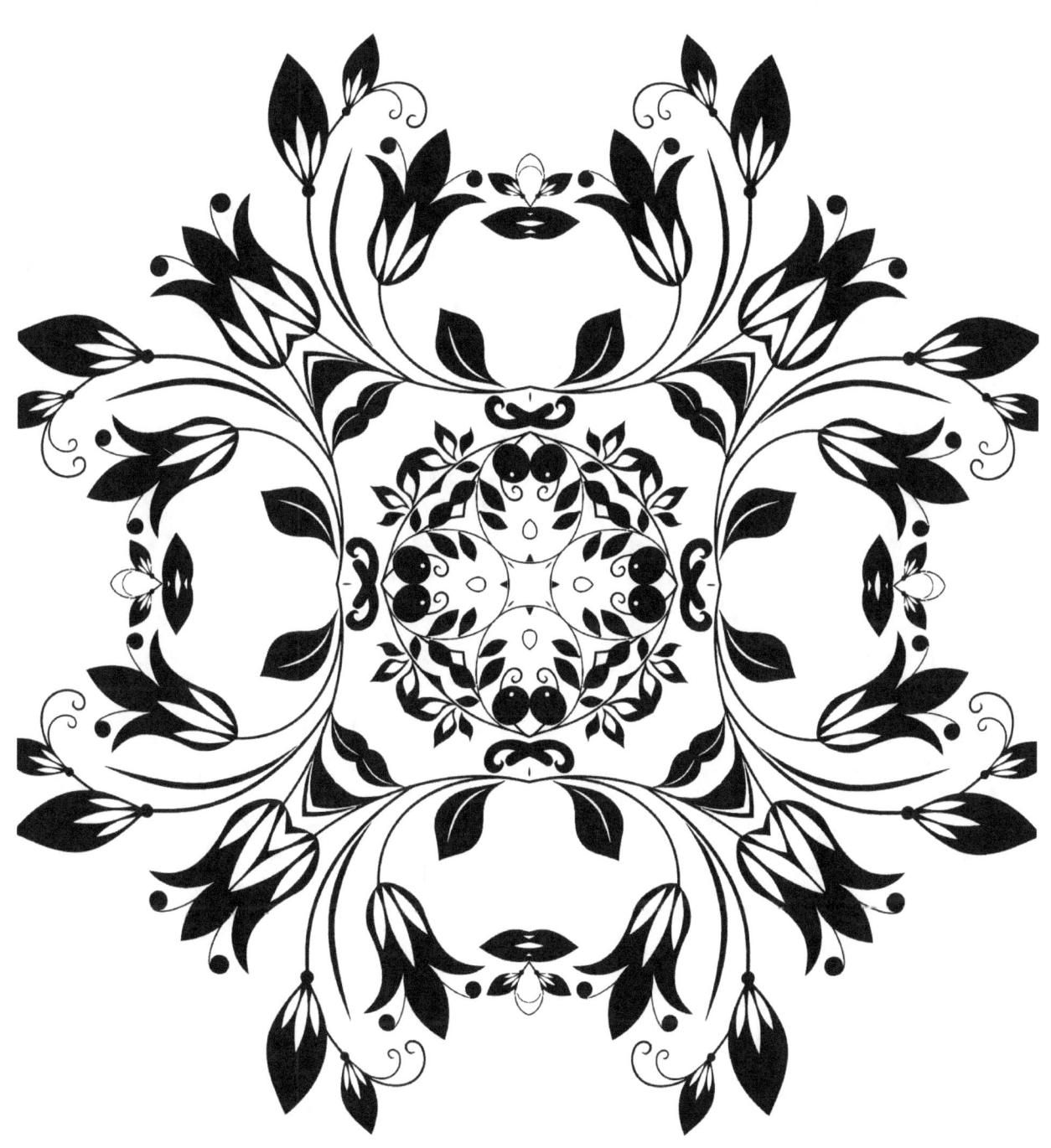

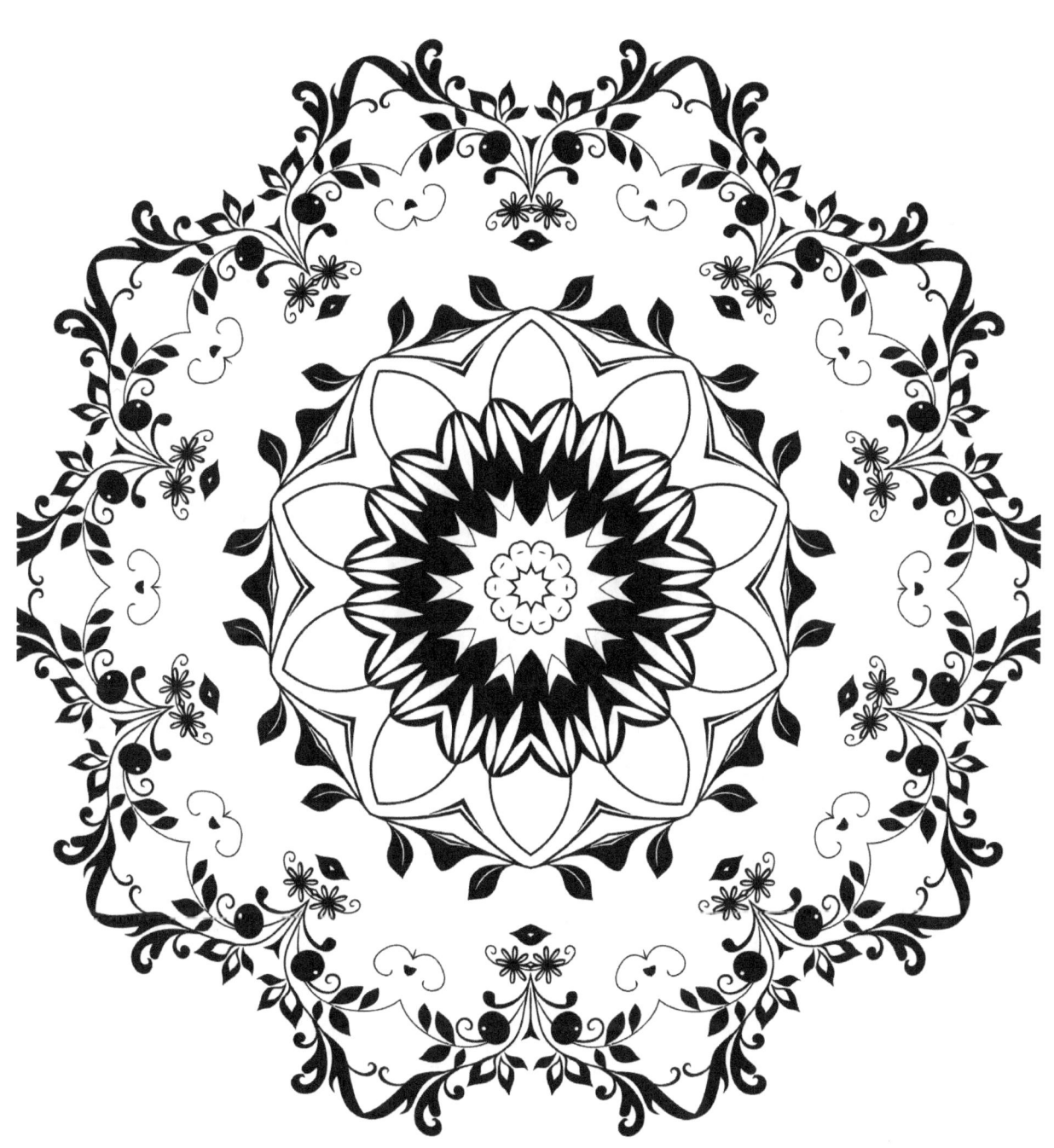

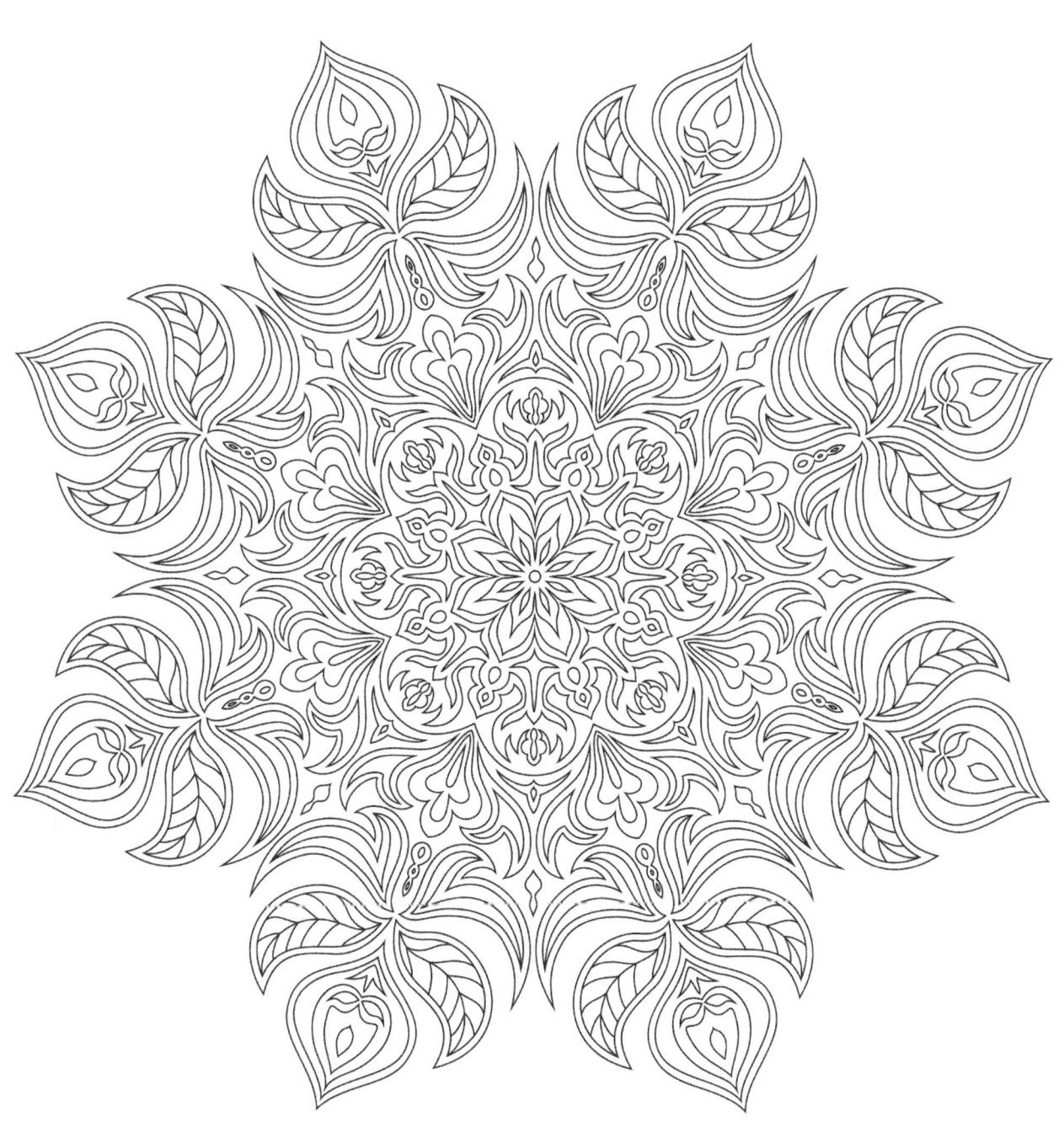

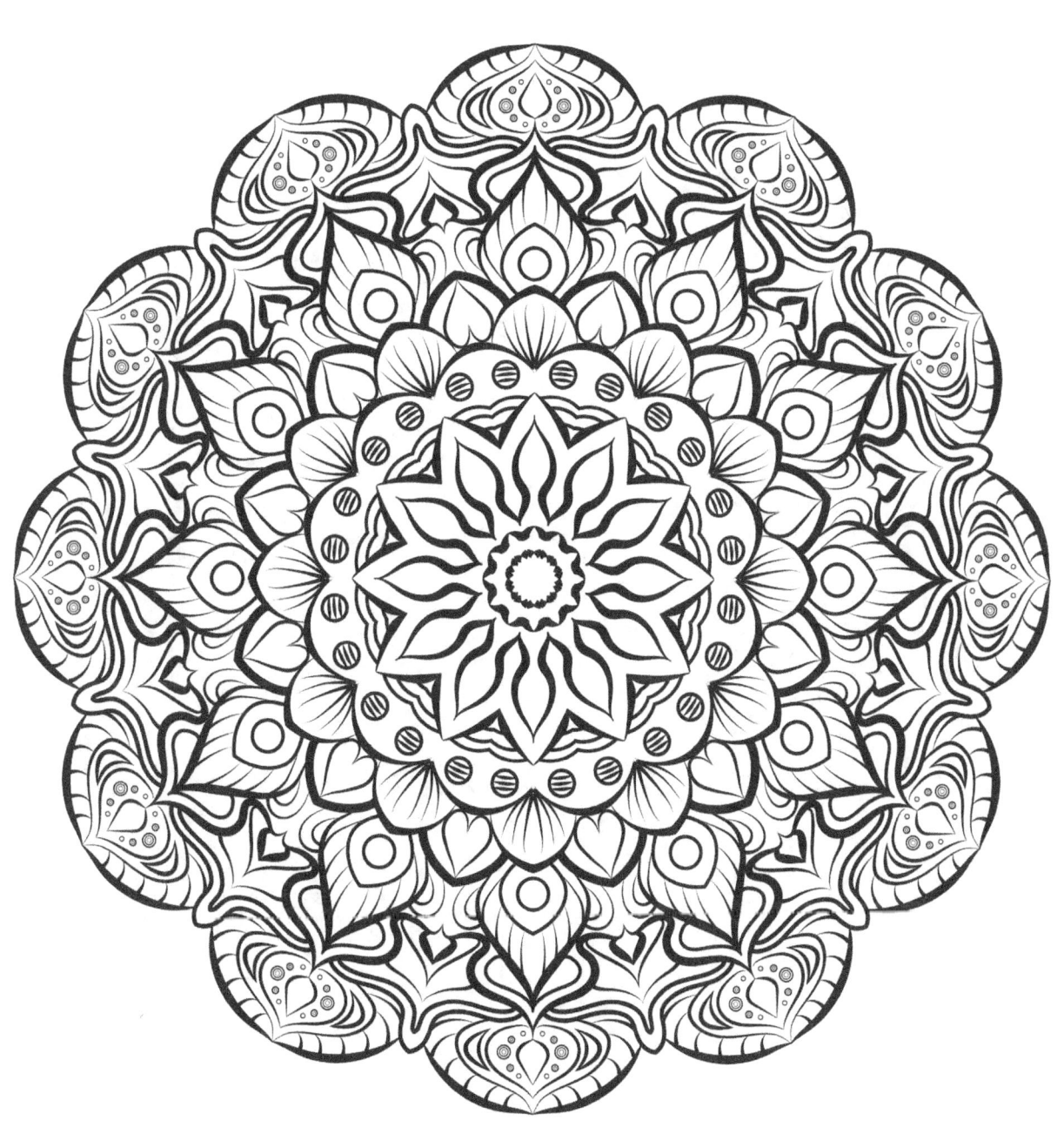

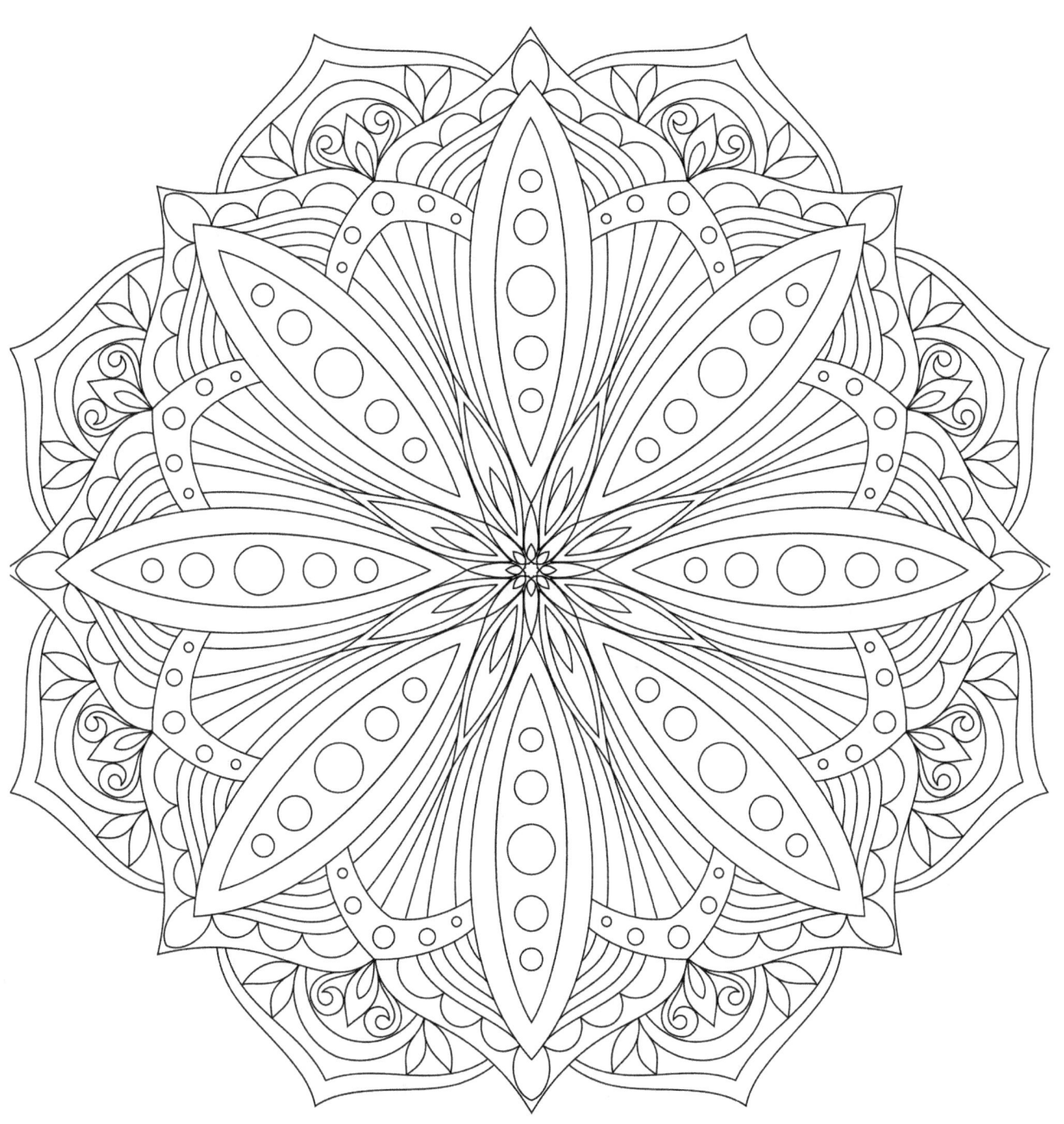

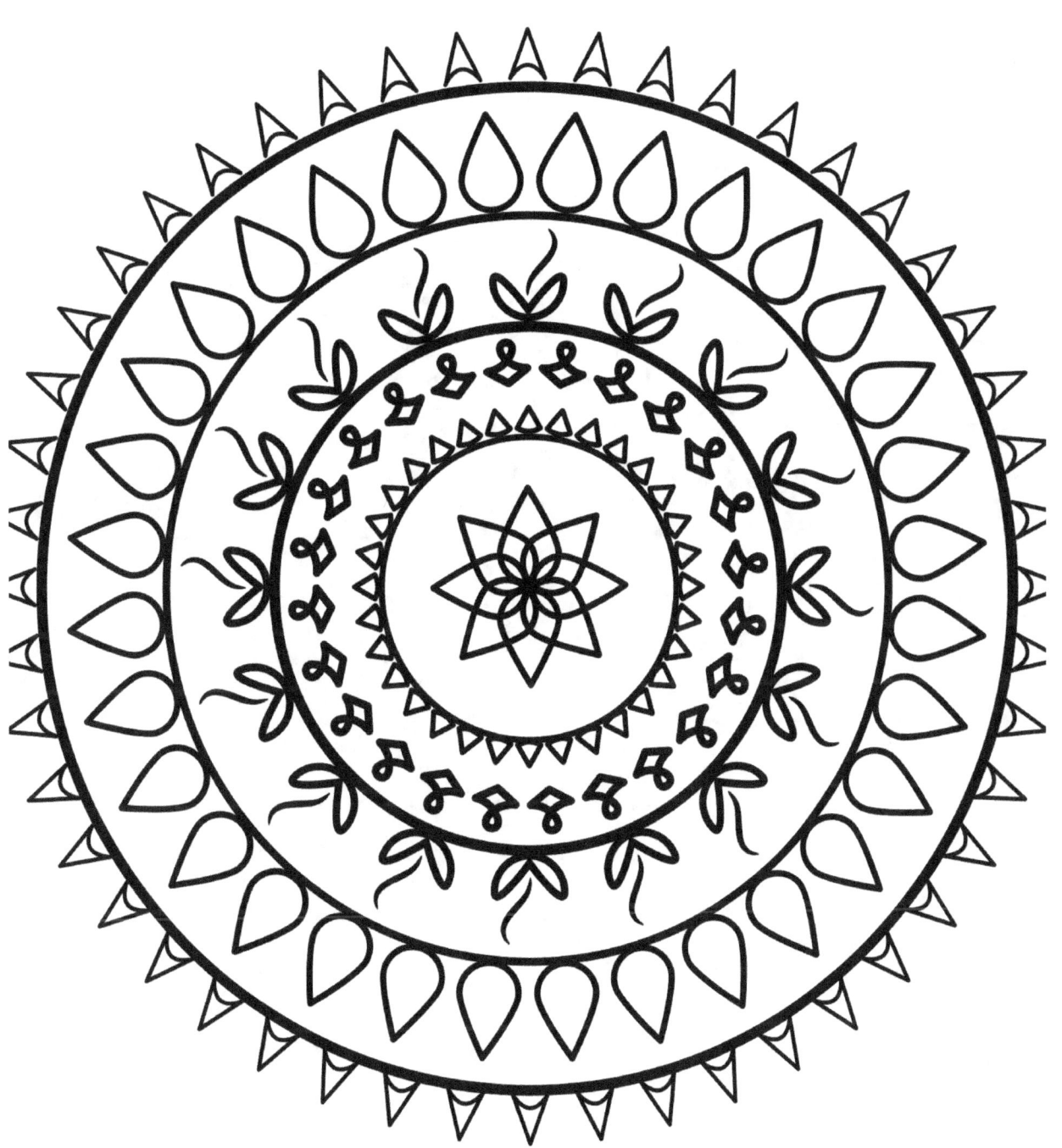

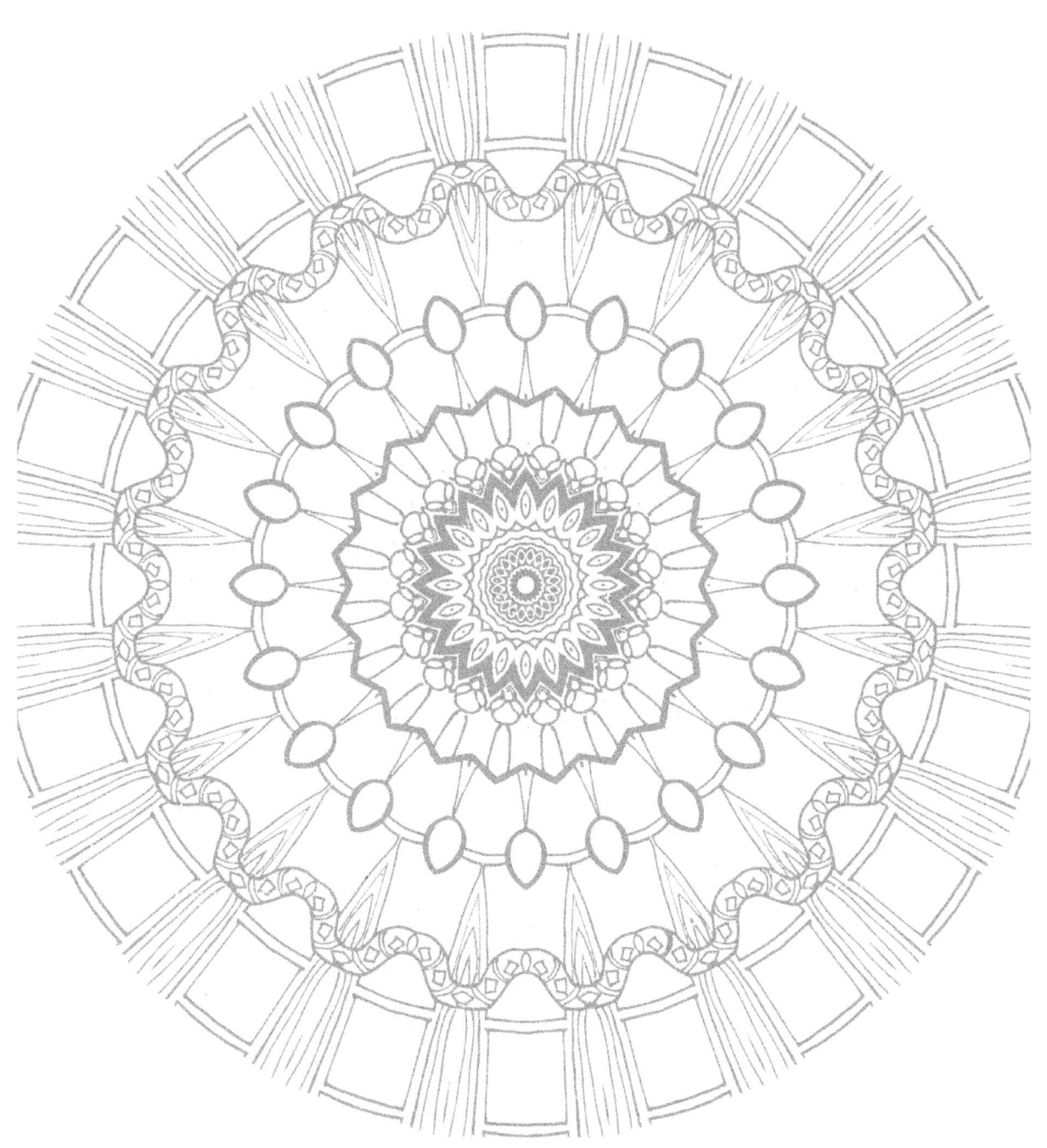

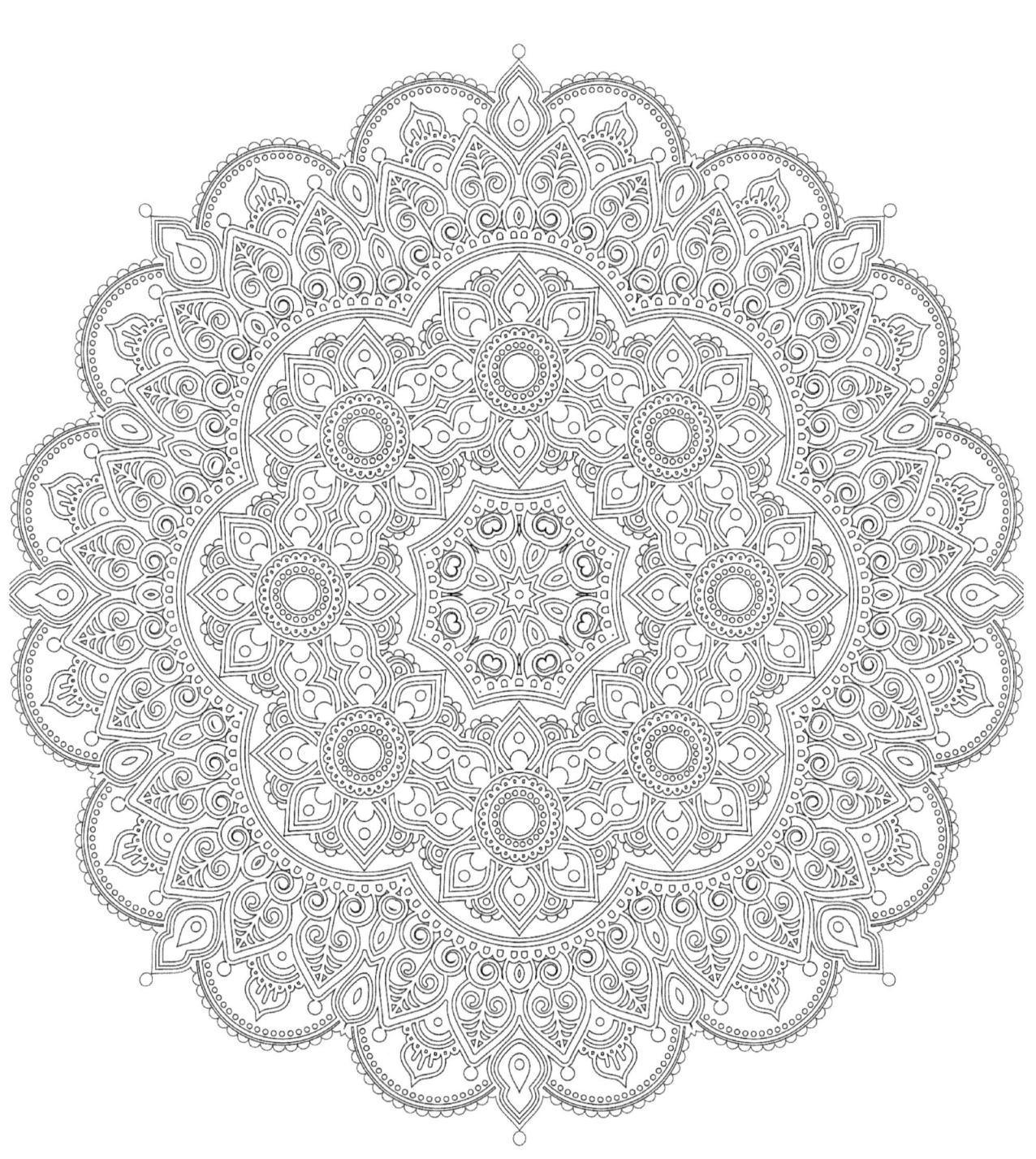

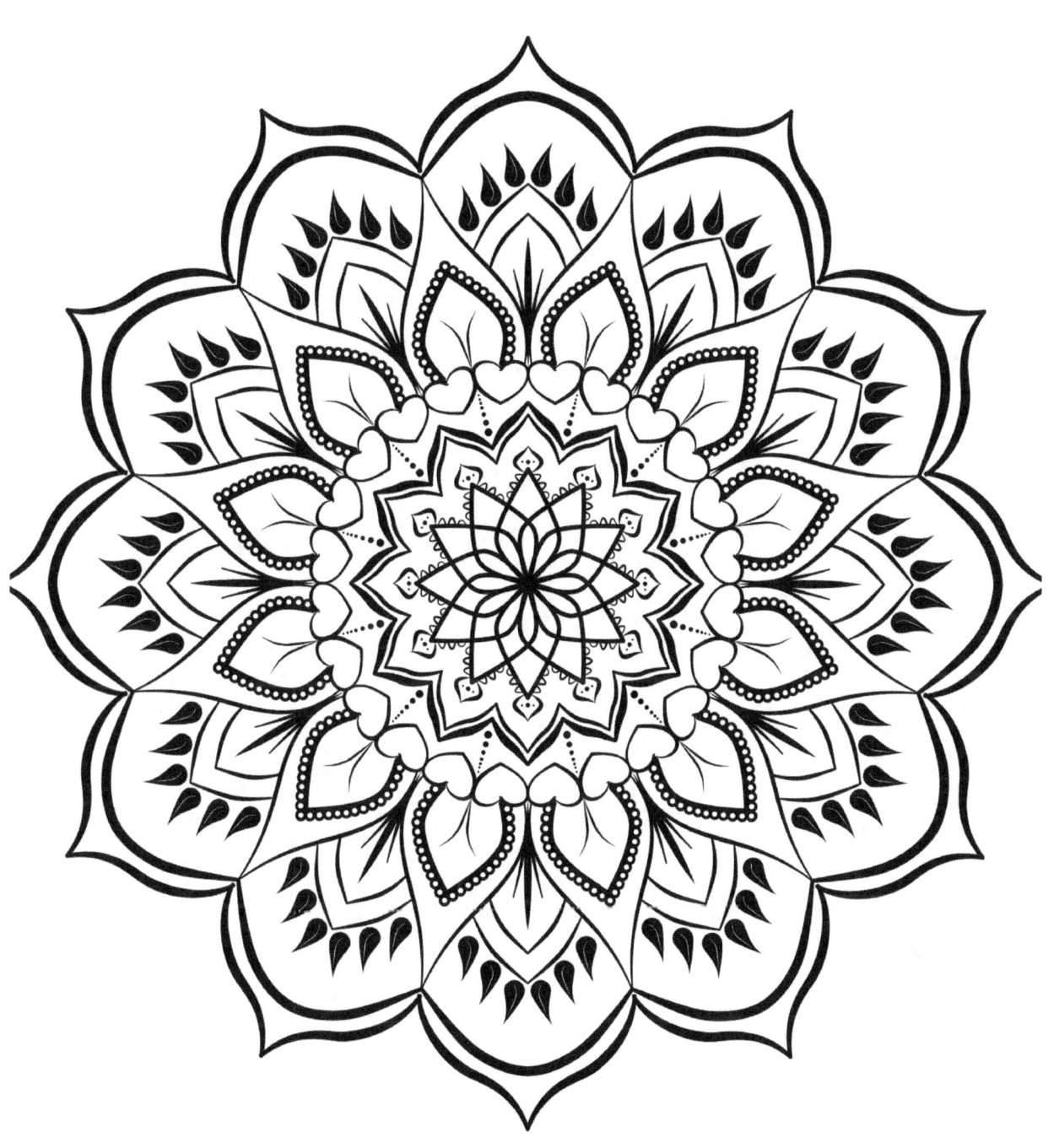

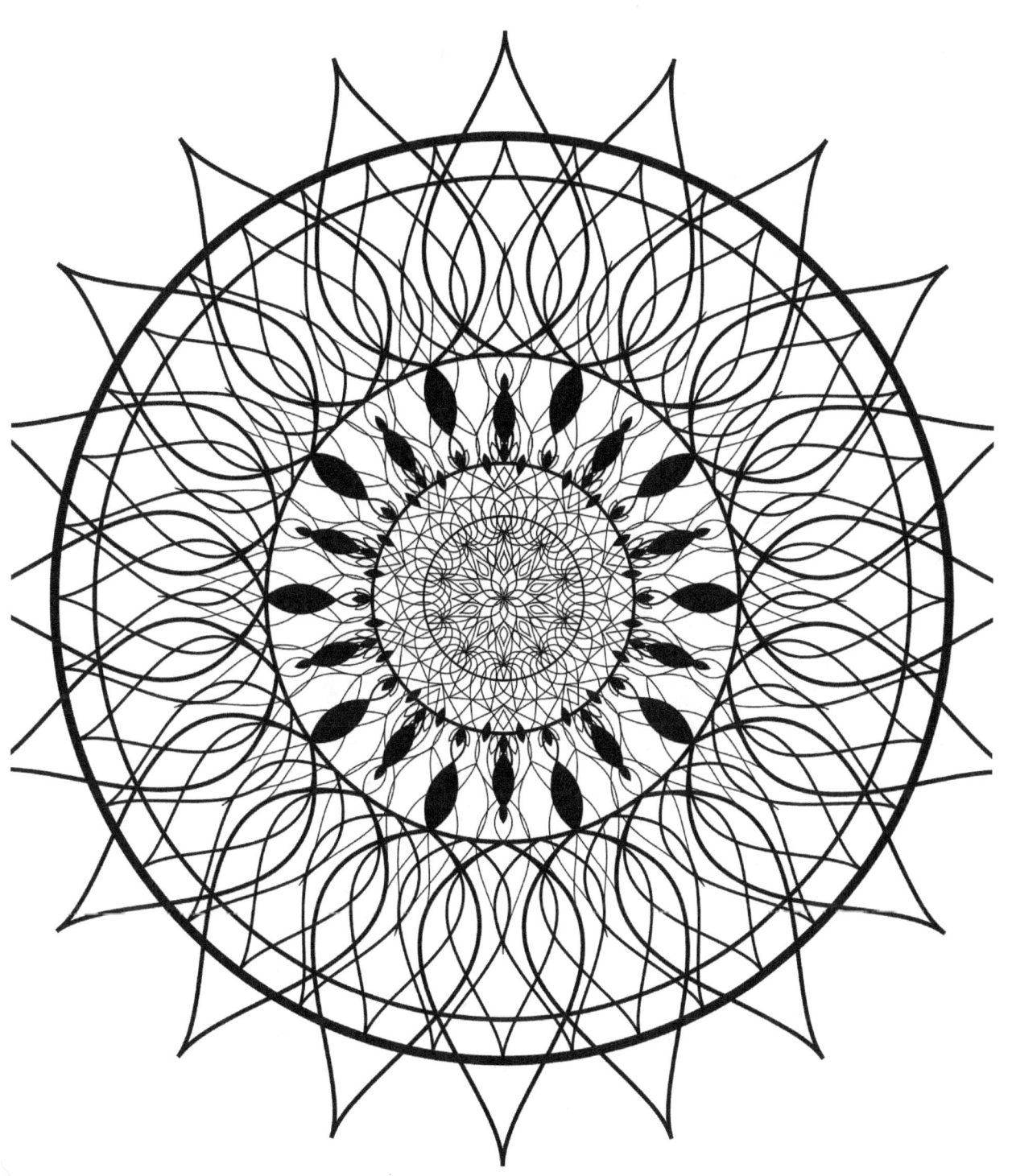

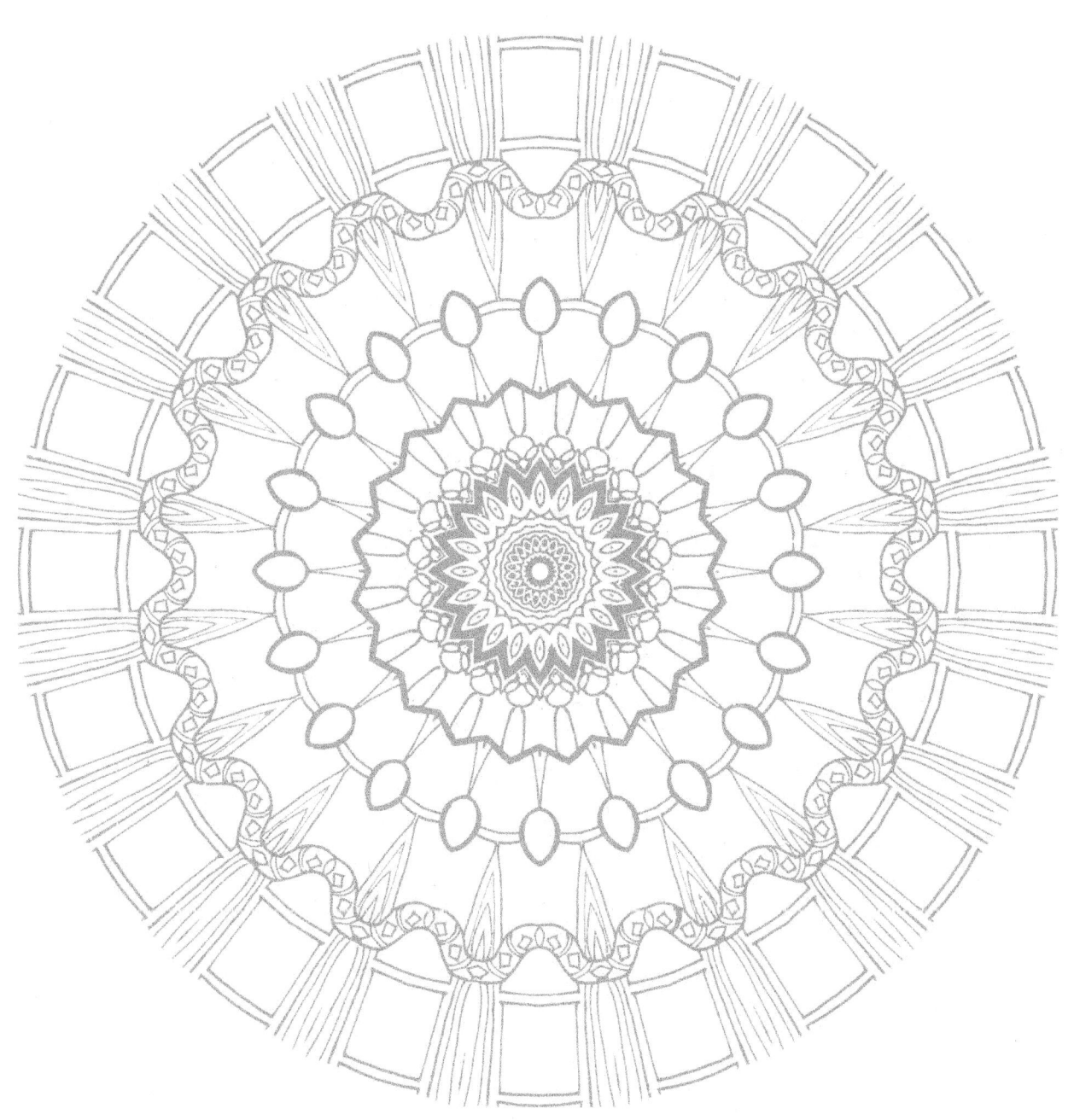

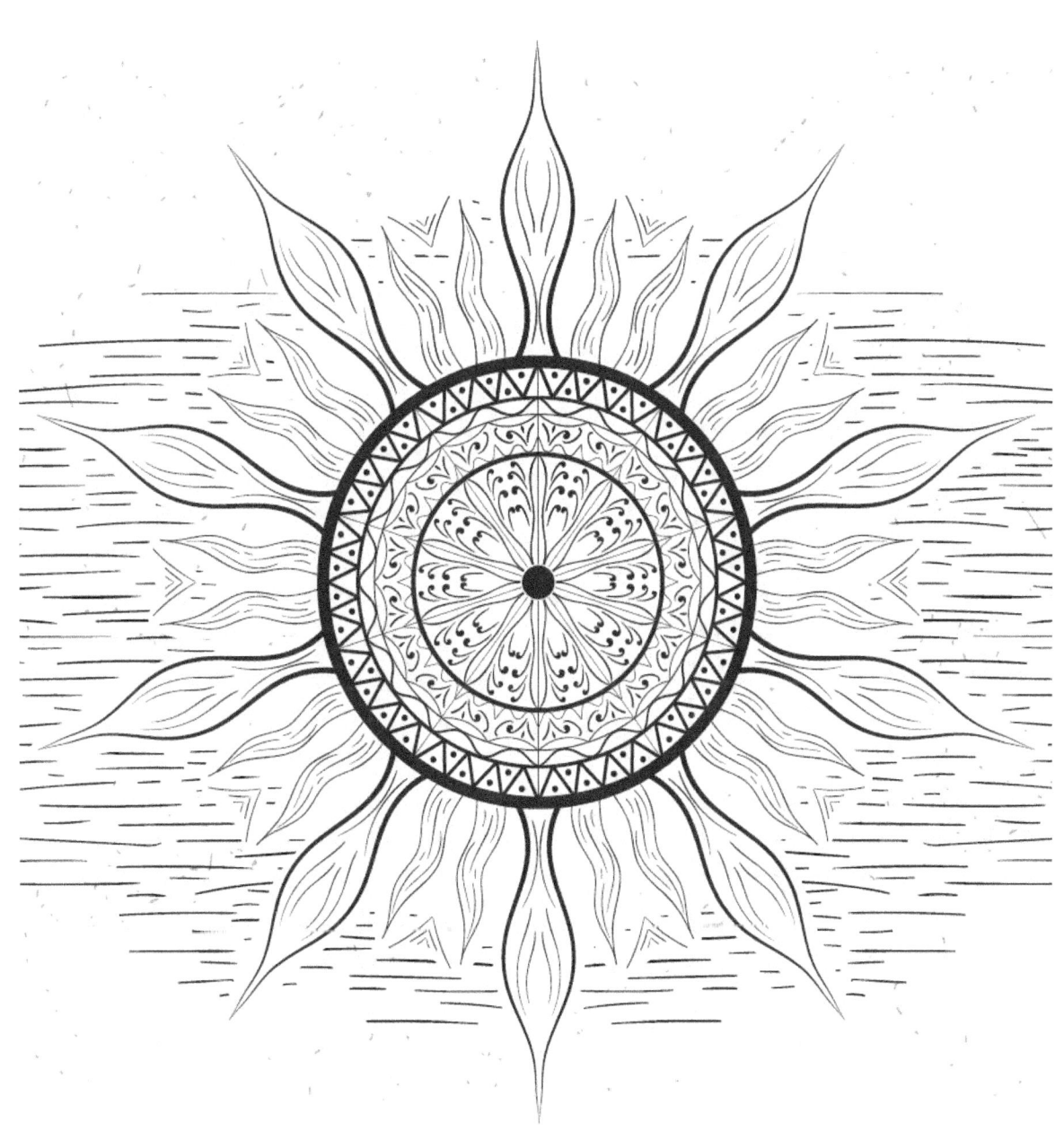

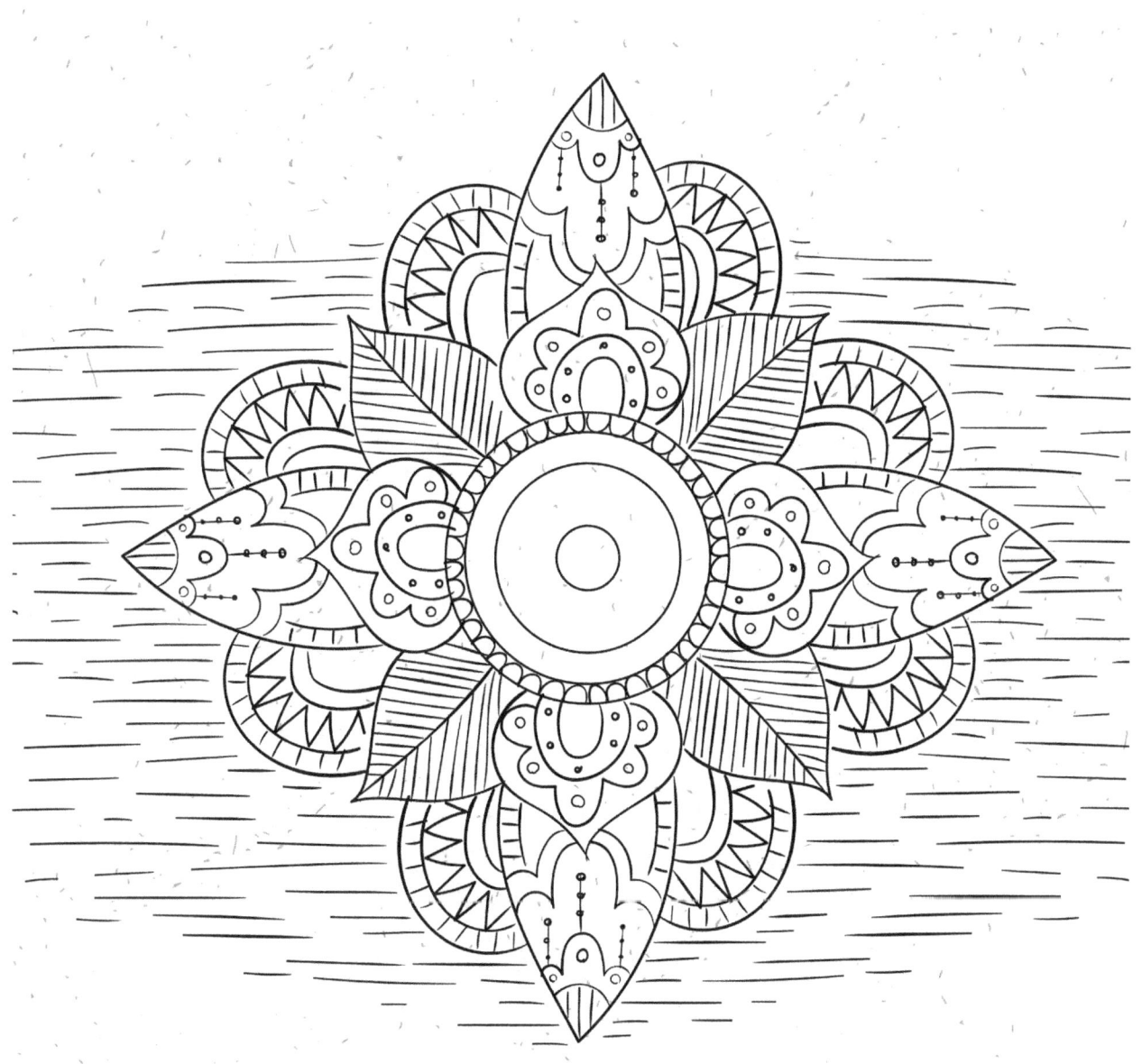

16 animals Photo with mandala: for adults with mandala animals (lions, elephants, owls, horses, dogs, cats and many more!)

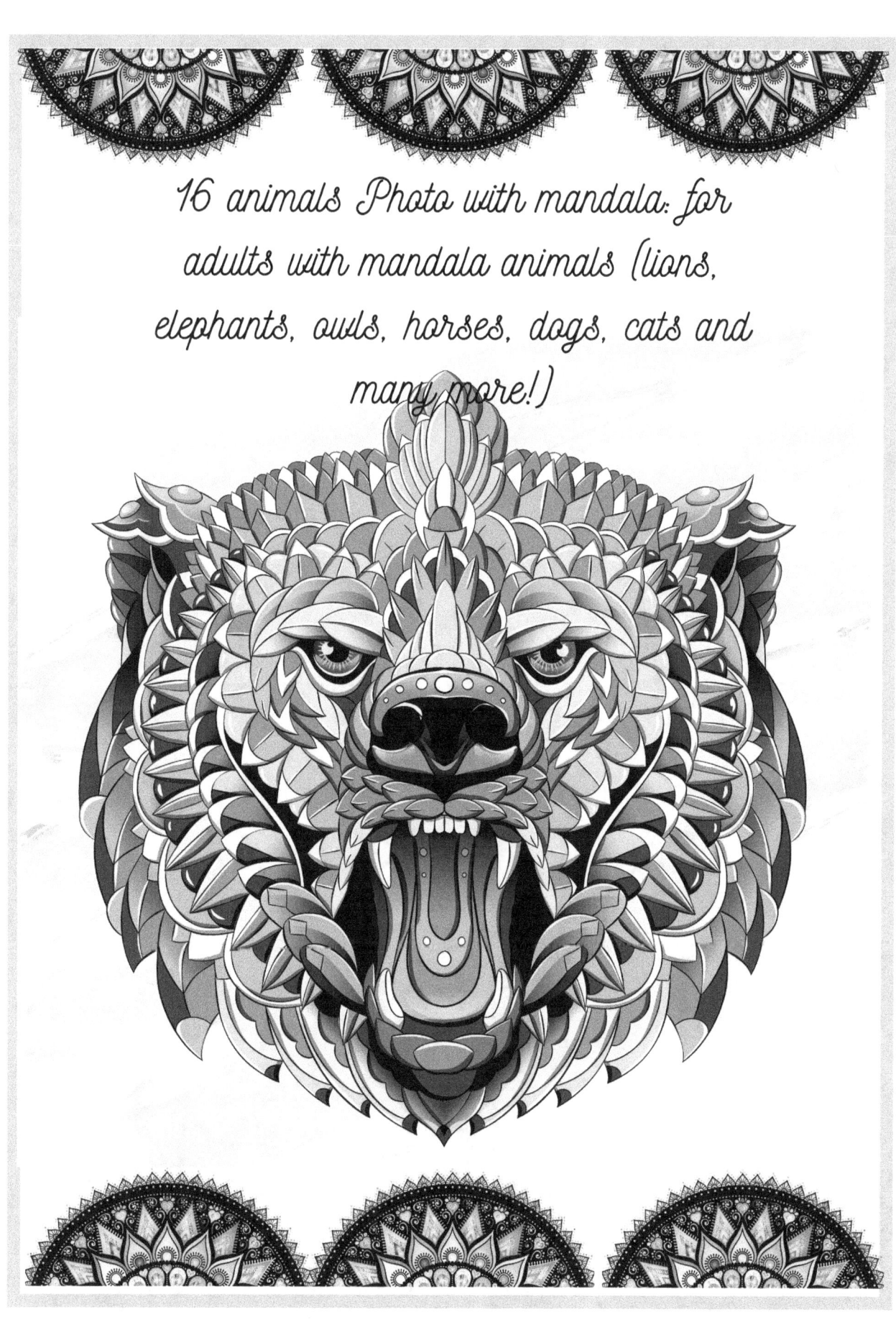

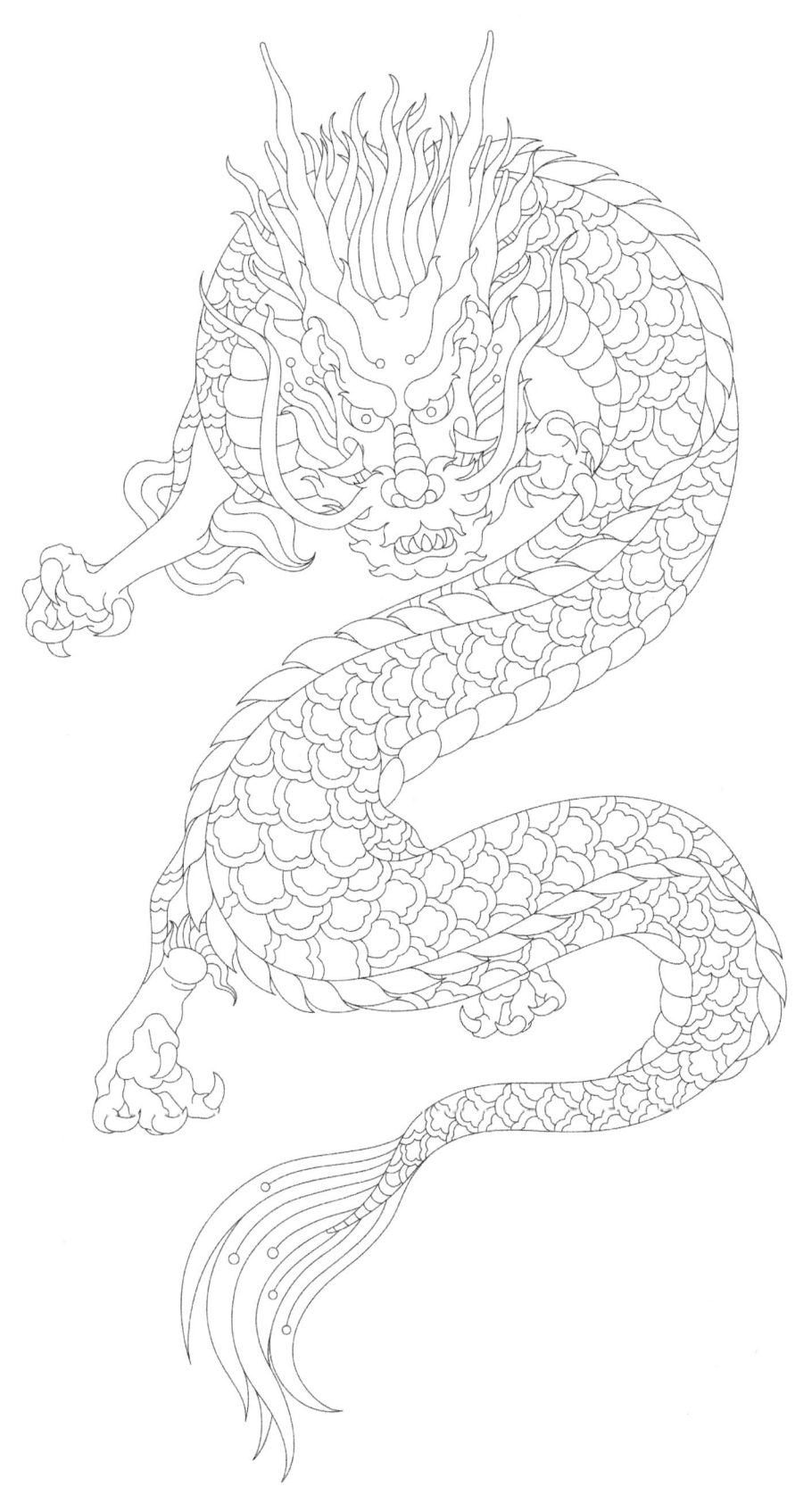

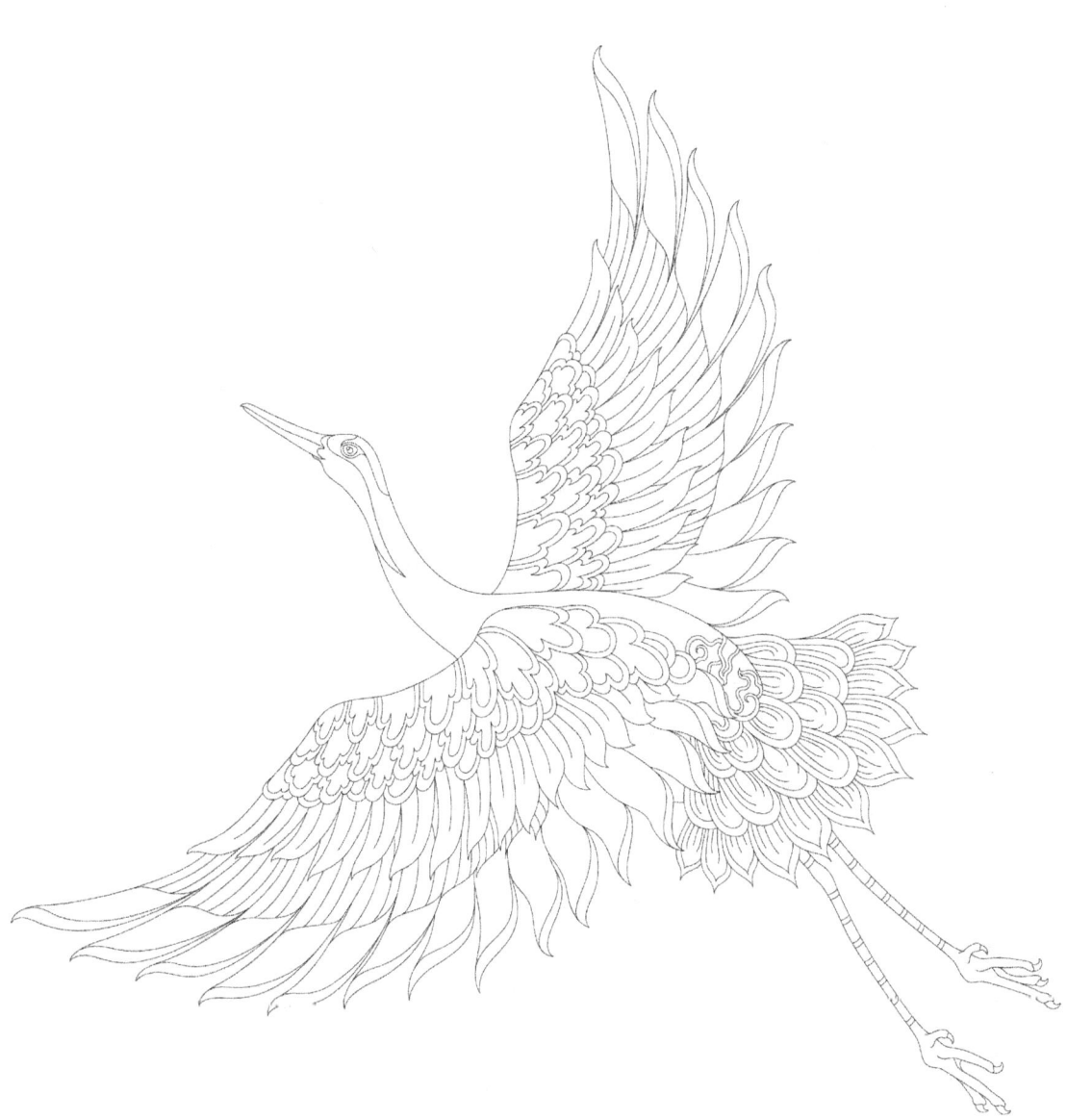

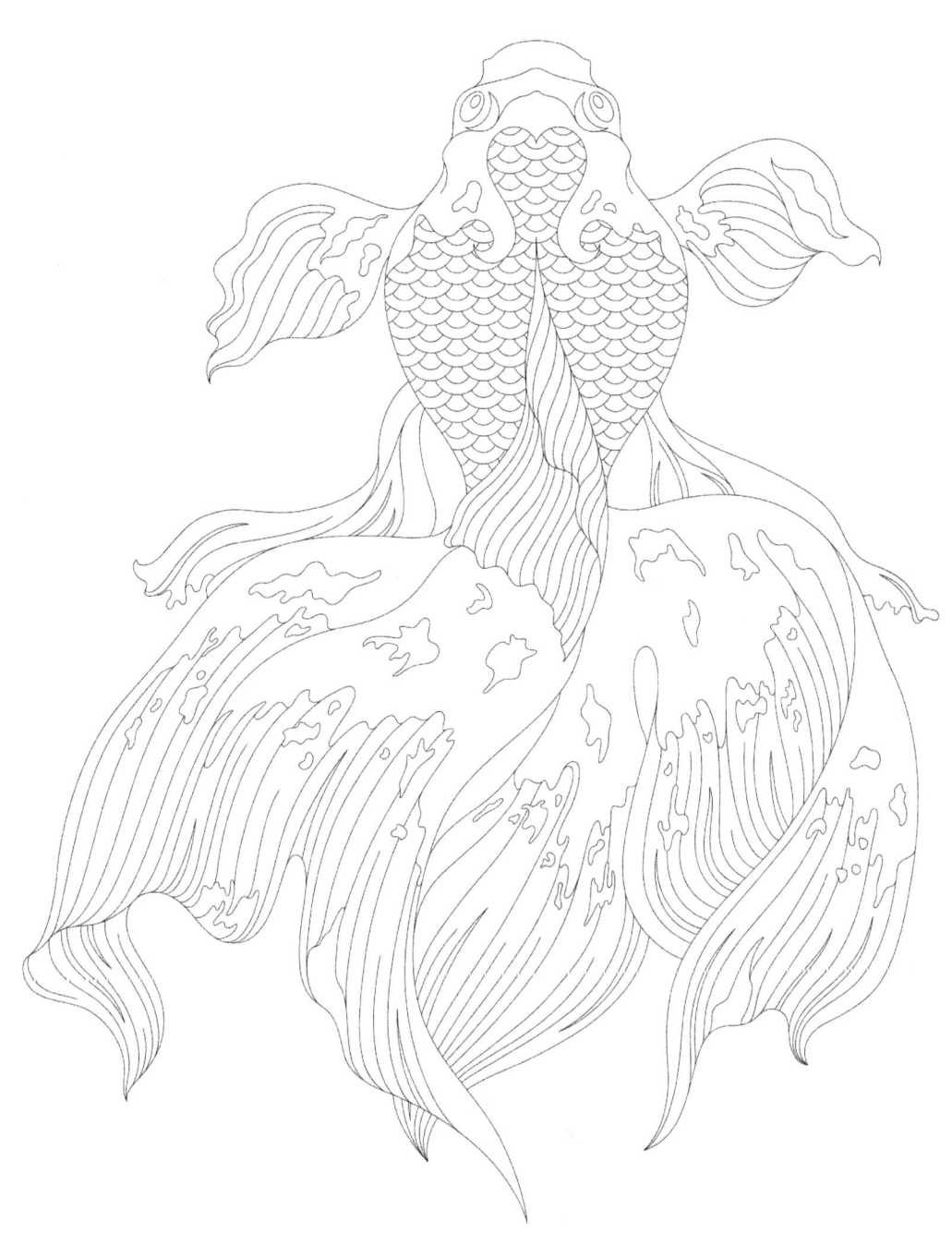

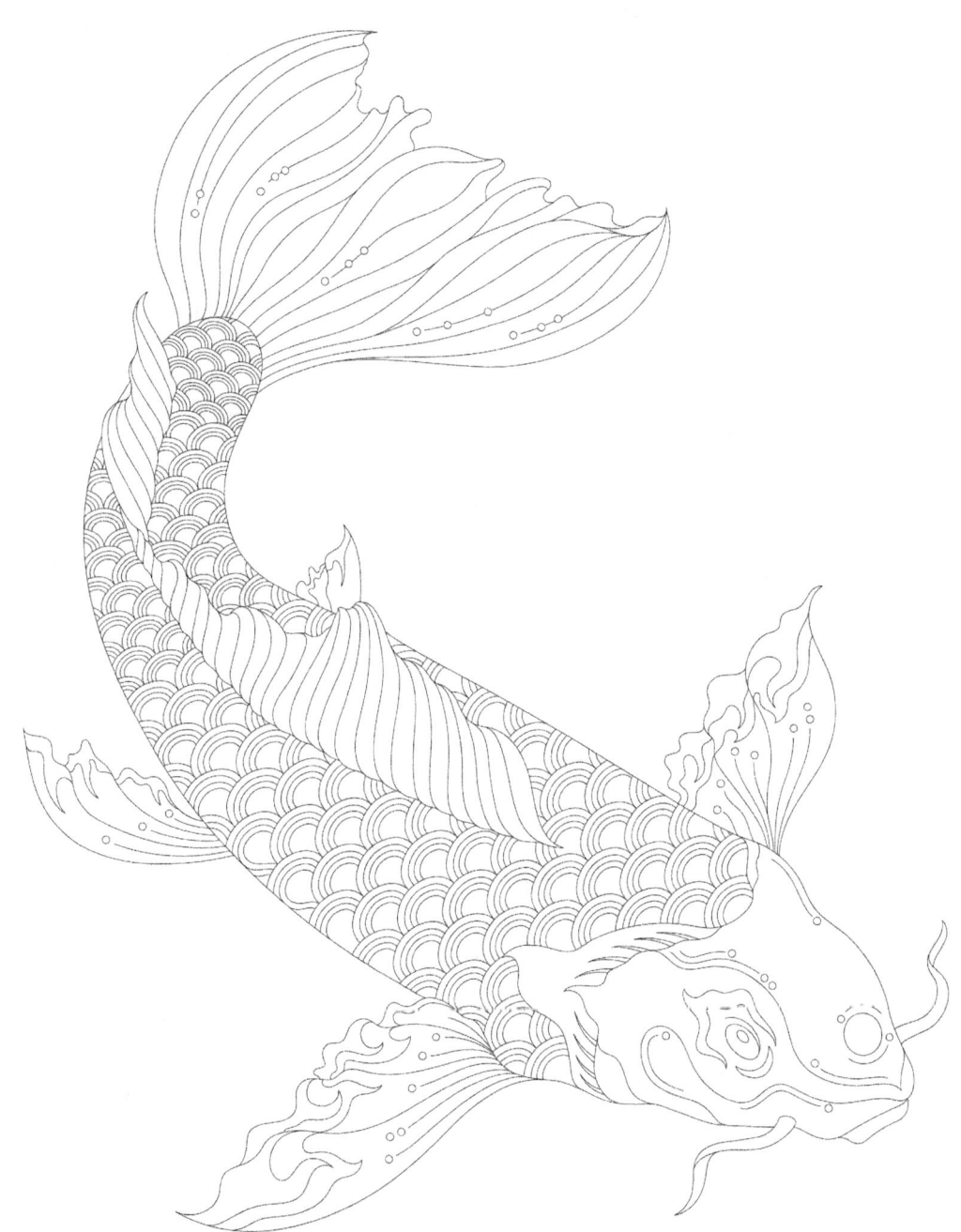

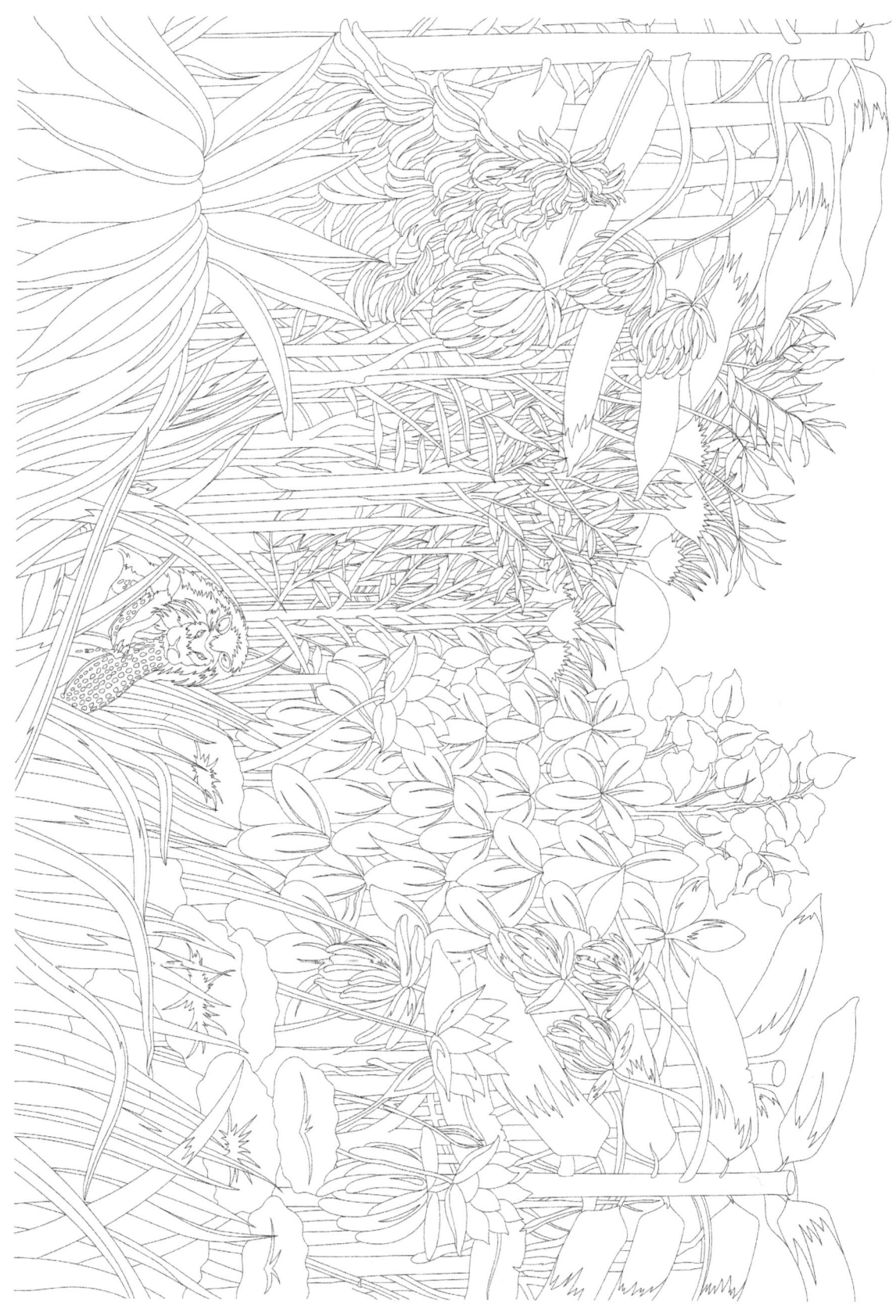

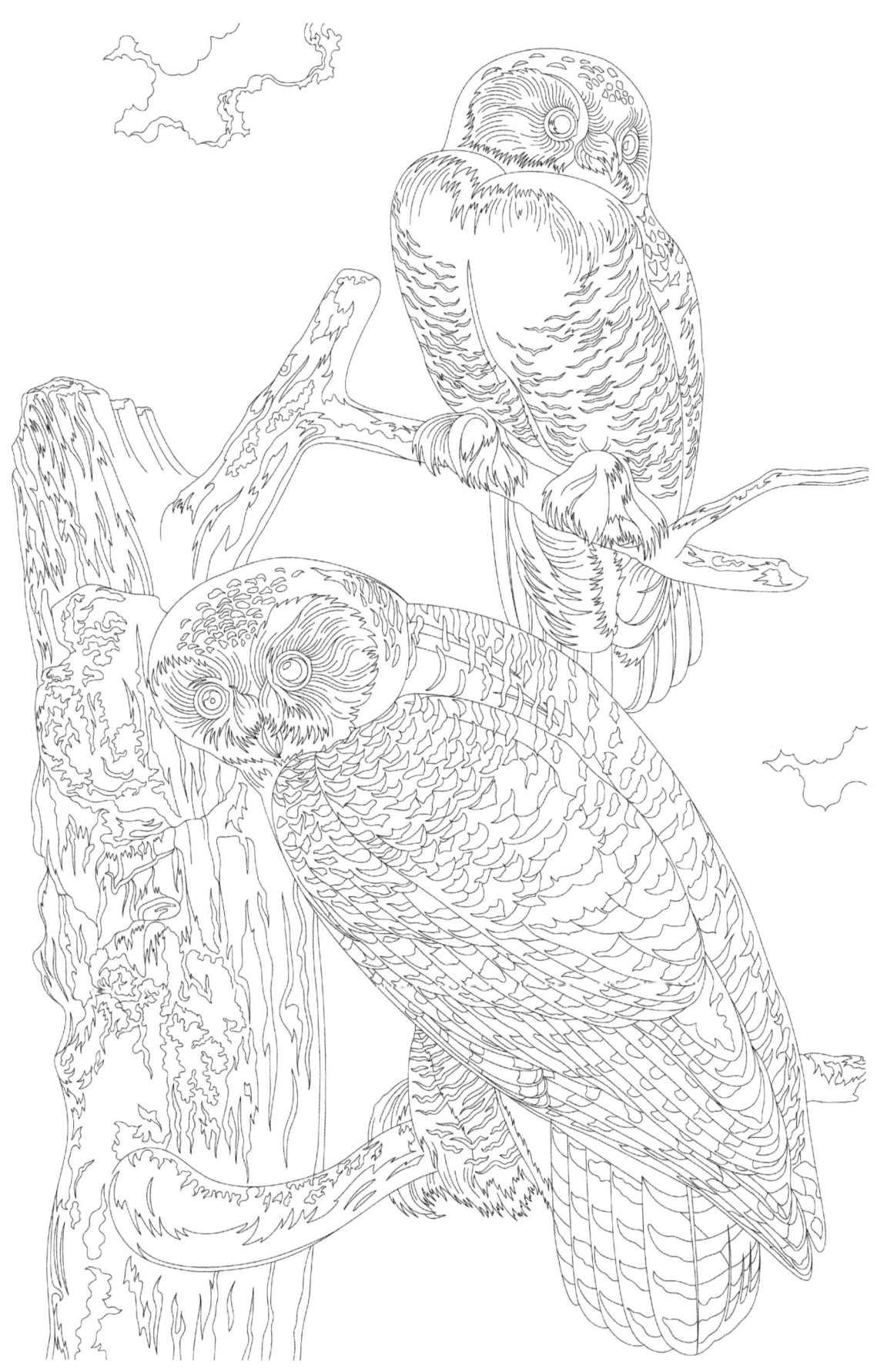

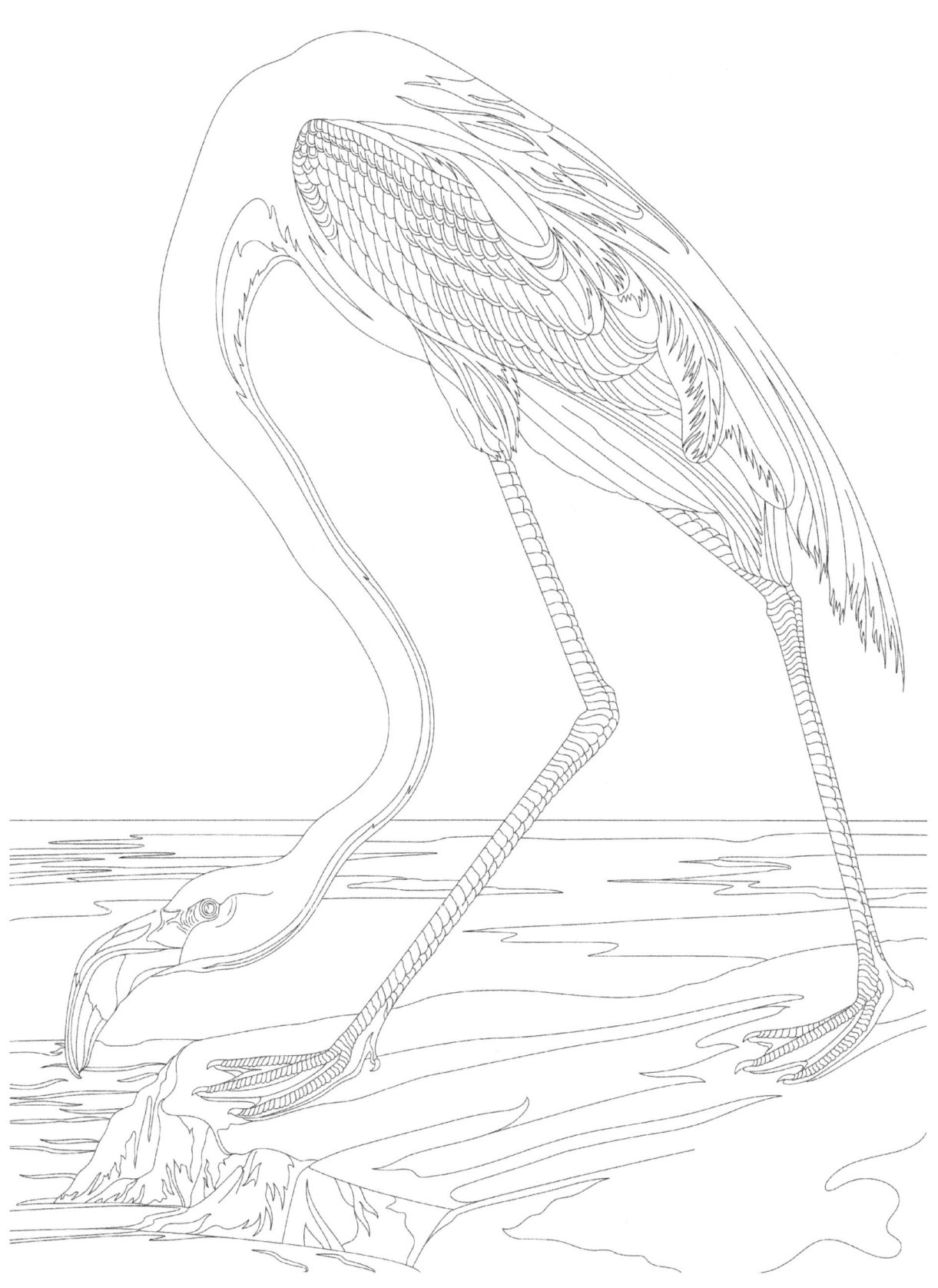

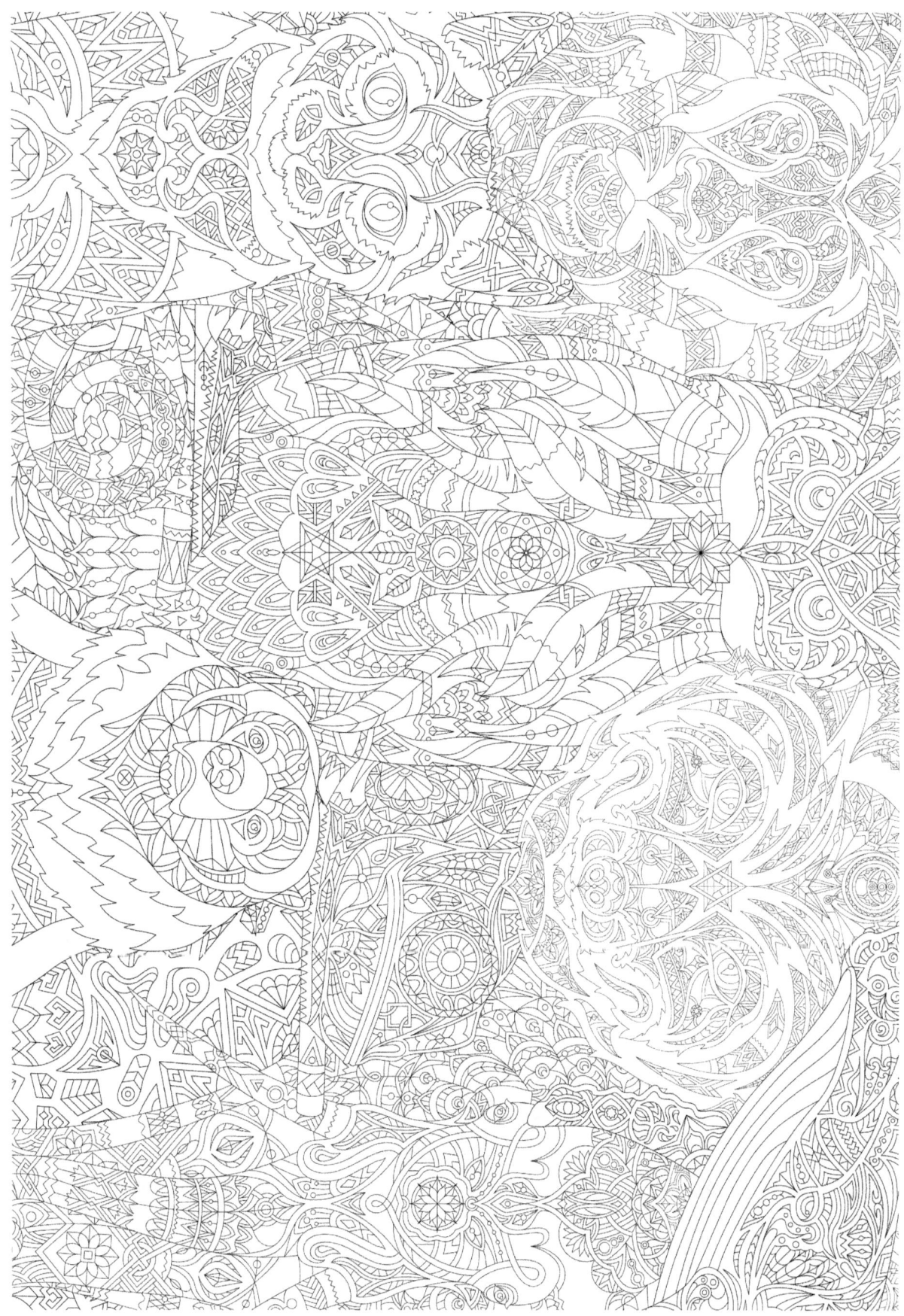

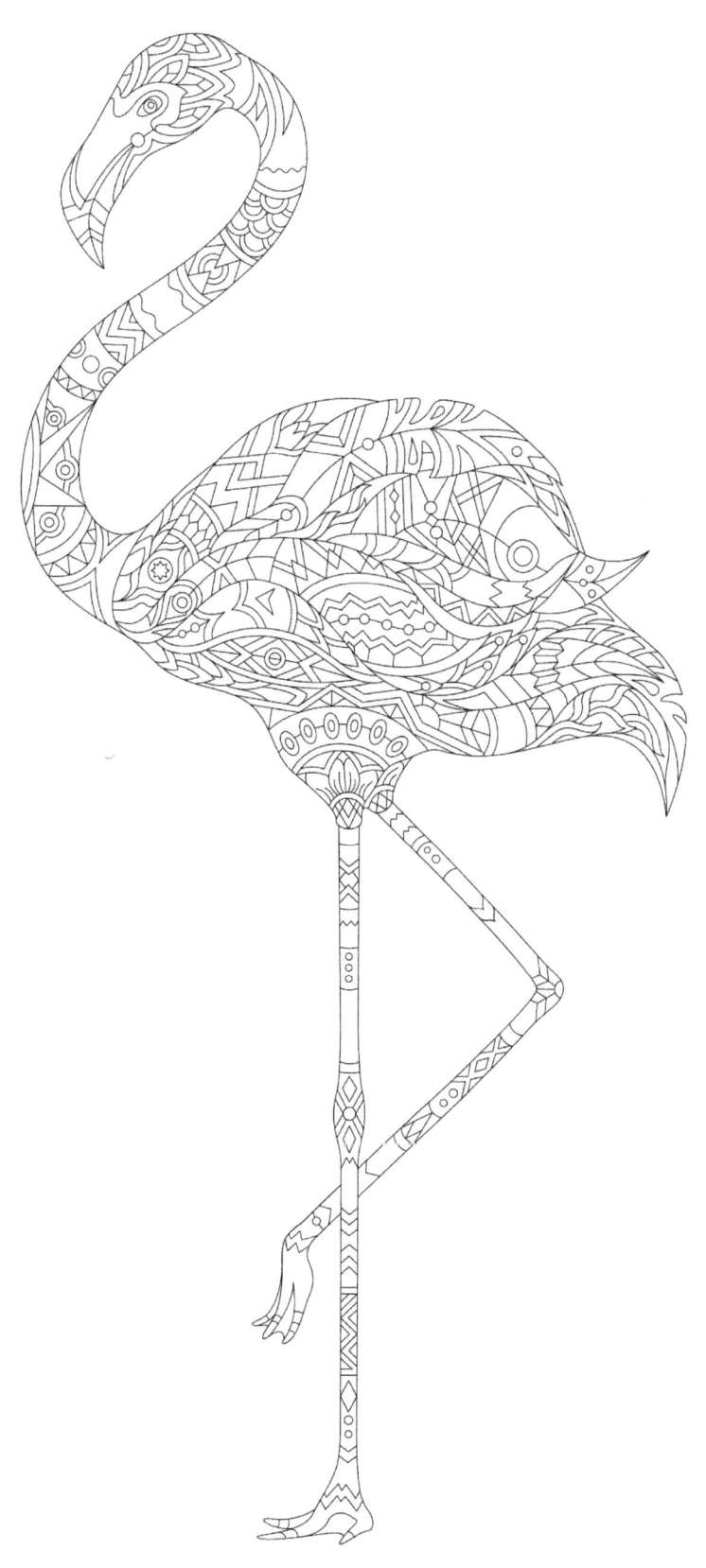

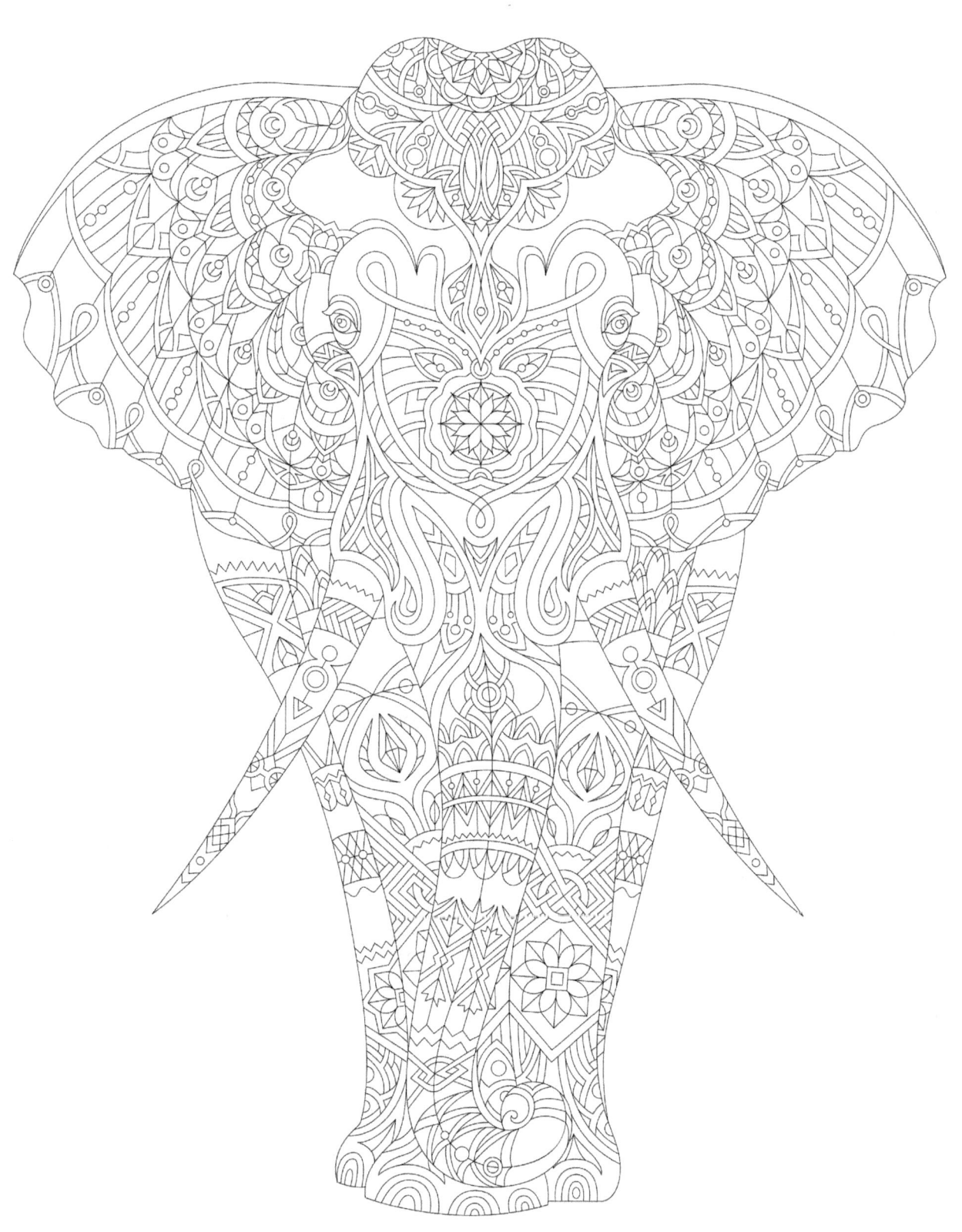

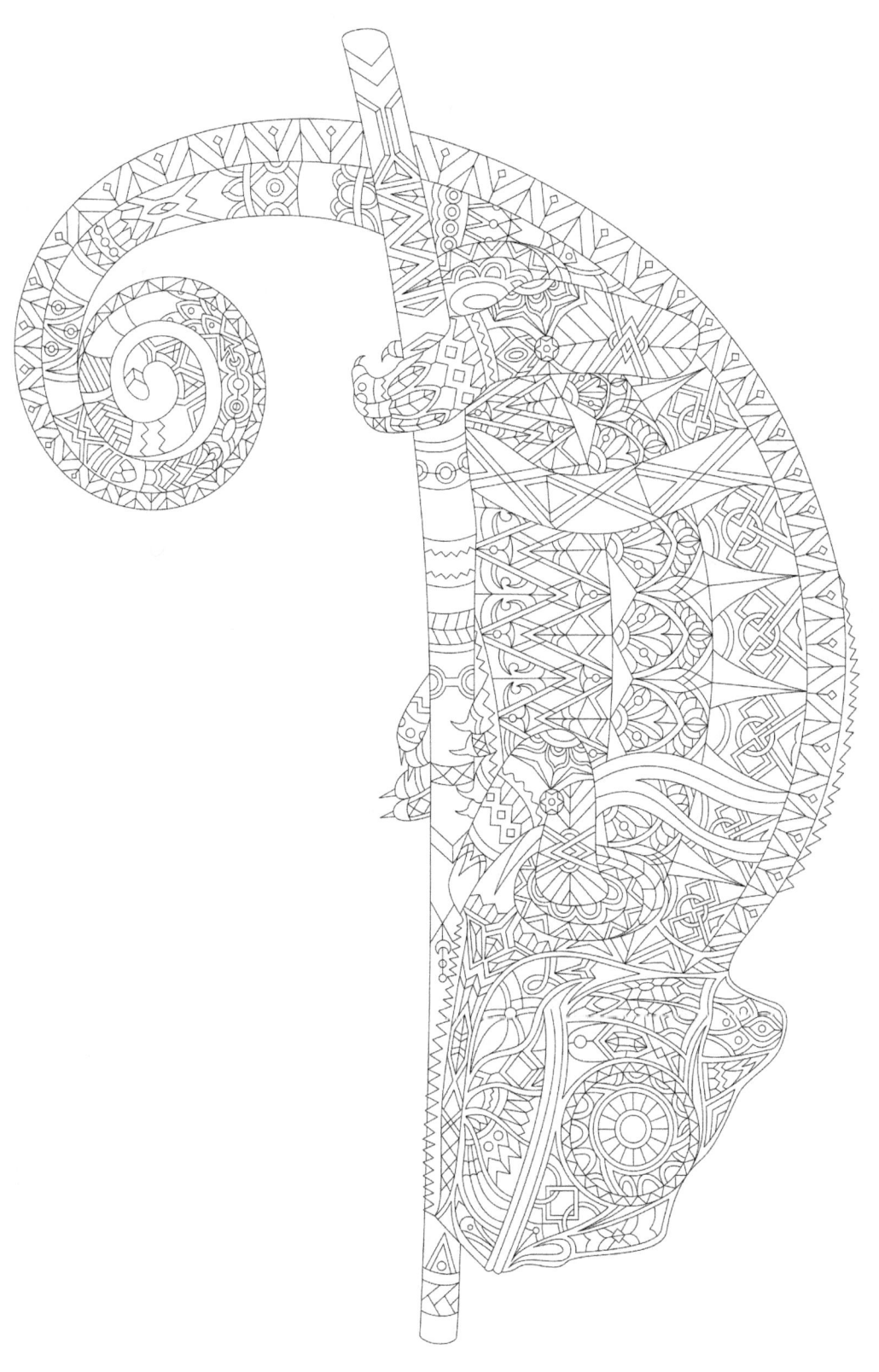

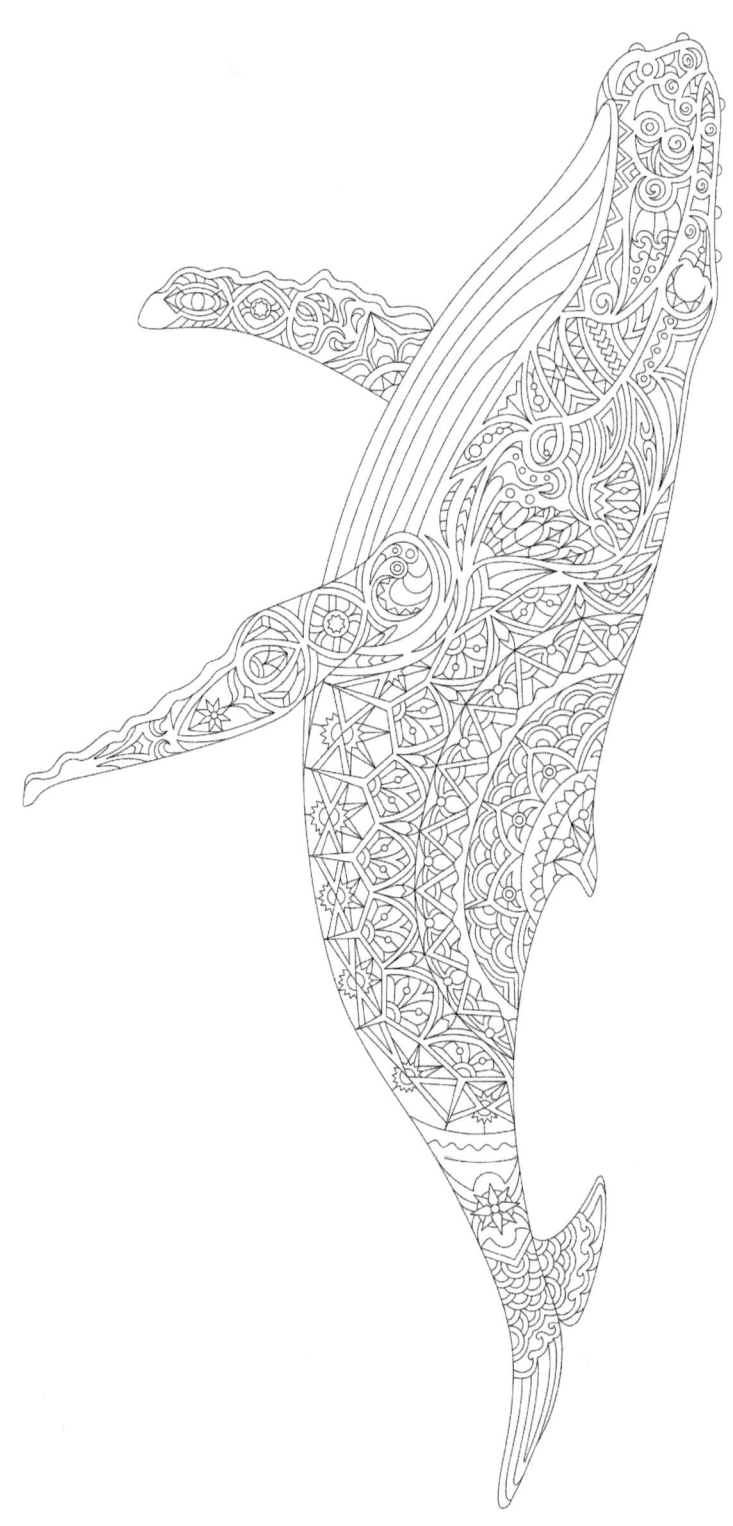

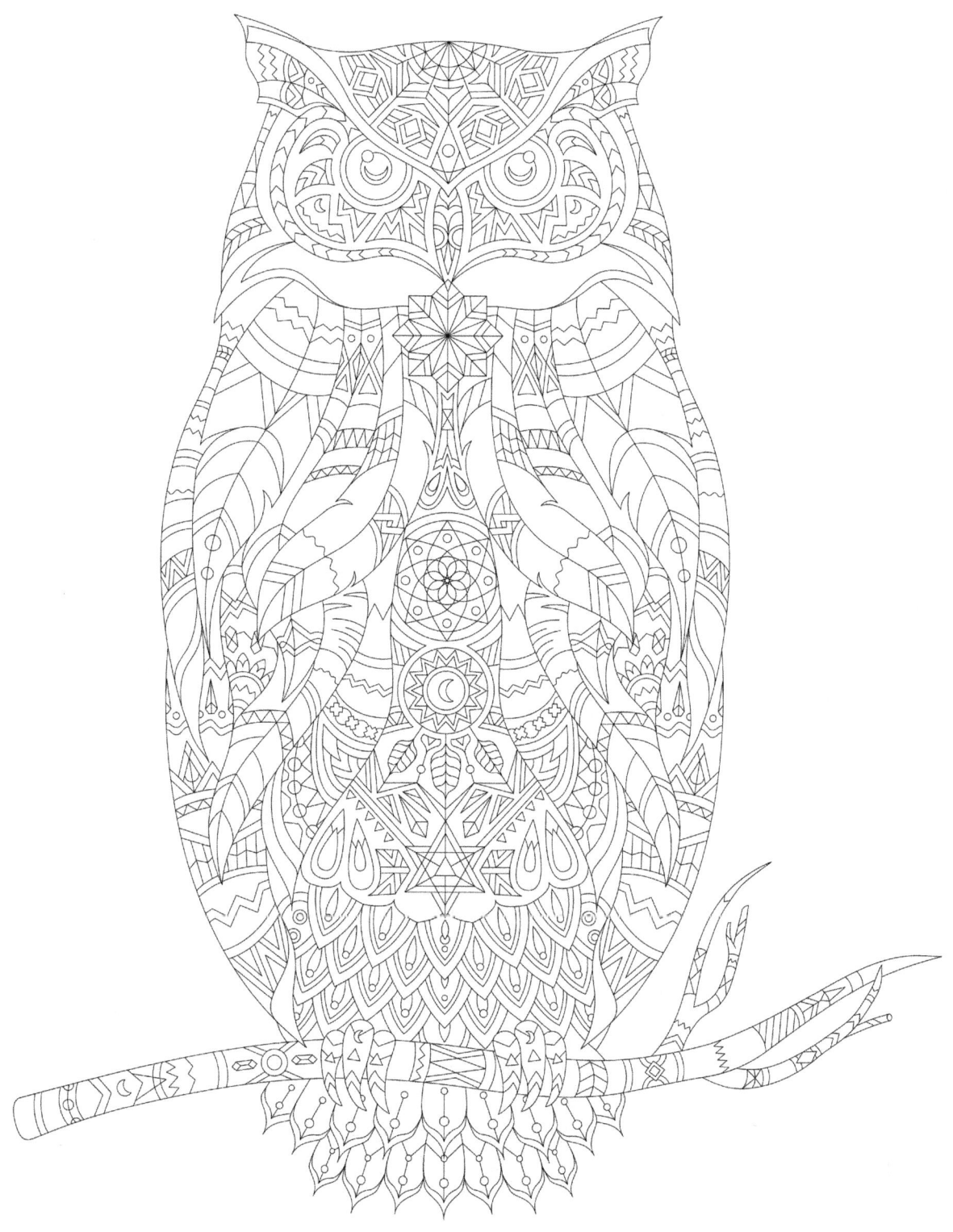

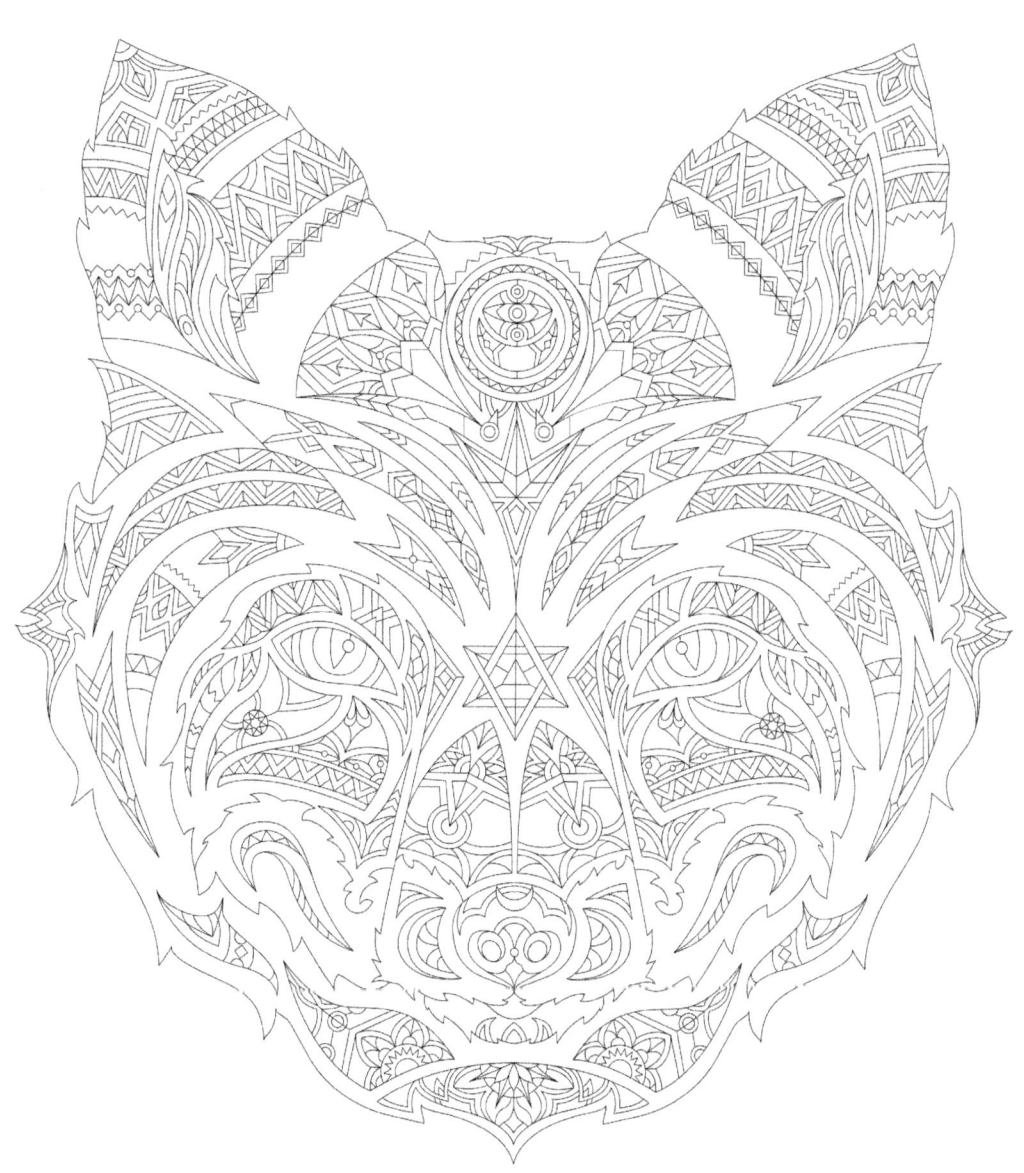

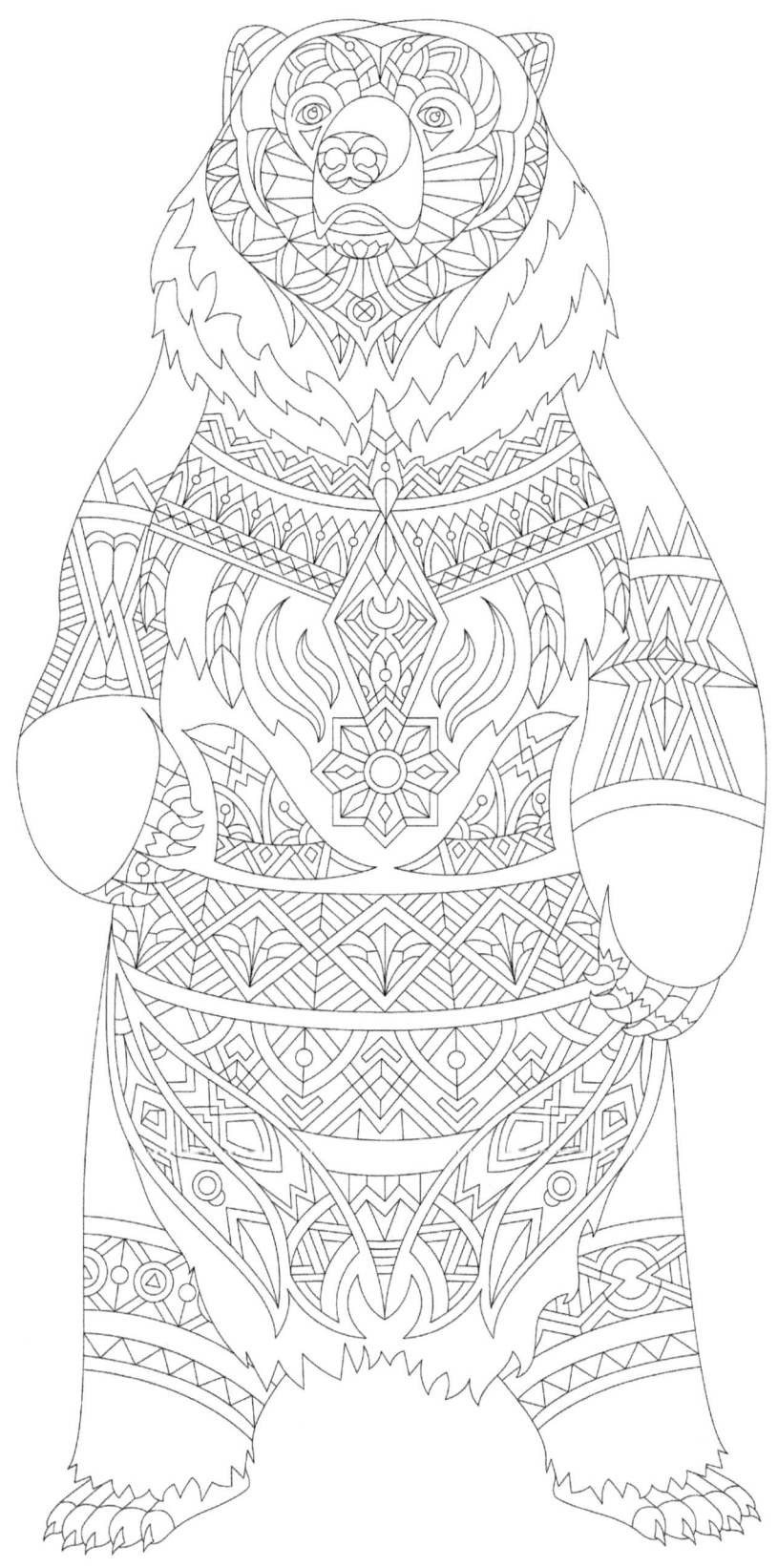

www.ingramcontent.com/pod-product-compliance
Lightning Source LLC
Chambersburg PA
CBHW081057240526
45465CB00025B/2464